C-SPAN

Traveling Tocqueville's America

C-SPAN

Traveling Tocqueville's America

Retracing the 17-state tour that inspired

Alexis de Tocqueville's political classic

Democracy in America

Published for C-SPAN® by
The Johns Hopkins University Press
Baltimore and London

A C-SPAN® publication

C-SPAN, the Cable Satellite Public Affairs Network, was created by the cable industry as a public service to provide unedited and balanced access to the political process. The networks are funded by the cable industry, without government or taxpayer support, and provide gavel-to-gavel coverage of the U.S. House and Senate, hearings, press conferences, campaign coverage and book programming. C-SPAN® is a registered service mark of the National Cable Satellite Corporation.

The information in this book has been carefully researched; however, locations, attractions and phone numbers are subject to change. The publisher cannot take responsibility for changes. Travelers are encouraged to call to verify information.

The Johns Hopkins University Press
2715 North Charles Street
Baltimore, Maryland 21218-4363
The Johns Hopkins Press Ltd., London
www.press.jhu.edu

Written by Anne Bentzel
Edited by Scott Ingram, Karen Jarmon, John Splaine and Susan Swain
Researched by Ed Aymar, Marybeth Murphy and Erika Robinson
Cover and book design by Margret Lloyd

Library of Congress Cataloging-in-Publication Data

Traveling Tocqueville's America : retracing the 17-state tour that
    inspired Alexis de Tocqueville's political classic, Democracy in
    America.
        p.   cm.
    At head of title: C-SPAN.
    Includes bibliographical references (p.   ).
    ISBN 0-8018-5965-4 (alk. paper). — ISBN 0-8018-5966-2 (pbk. :
alk. paper)
    1. United States—Tours. 2. Tocqueville, Alexis de, 1805–1859 —Journeys—
United States. I. C-SPAN (Television network)
    E158.T77 1998
    917.304′5—DC21   98-9957
                                                                    CIP

A catalog record for this book is available from the British Library.

Contents

V

Foreword

"In that land the great experiment was to be made...for which the world had not been prepared by the history of the past."
     —Alexis de Tocqueville in *Democracy in America*

This book provides a way for contemporary travelers and history aficionados to follow the travels of Alexis de Tocqueville and Gustave de Beaumont when they visited America in 1831–32. C-SPAN (the Cable Satellite Public Affairs Network) retraced the Tocqueville journey over nine months, beginning in May of 1997 and televising, for a national audience, 55 of the stops Tocqueville made and discussing who he talked with in those locations and what he derived from his discussions and interviews.

Tocqueville and his companion, Beaumont, landed in Newport, Rhode Island on May 9, 1831. They left New York City aboard the same three-mast ship in which they arrived, the *Havre,* to sail back to their French homeland on February 20, 1832.

These two aristocrats from France had toured the United States for over nine months. This book chronicles the tour the two Frenchmen took which led to their respective books—Tocqueville's *Democracy in America* and Beaumont's fictional account of America's slave system, the novel *Marie.* This book allows readers to follow in their footsteps as the two friends conducted research for their classics.

Tocqueville and Beaumont, visiting America as commissioners for the French government, paid their own way to study the prison system in the United States; this was their government sanctioned reason for visiting the "new world." While in the United States, however, the French commissioners studied the new democratic society they found so they could bring back to France what they learned about this new way of conducting the government of a nation. Tocqueville, in particular, wanted the French to learn from American mistakes as well as successes.

In addition to studying the American mores and government, Tocqueville and Beaumont embarked on an adventure that would test them mentally and physically against the dangers inherent in traveling along and through the frontier. They explored, interviewed and studied in 17 of the then 24 states of the Union. As they crisscrossed state and nation, they encountered extreme heat, frigid temperatures, smothering humidity, swarming mosquitoes and ferocious-looking black bears acting as "watch dogs." Contemporary travelers can follow Tocqueville in those same 17 states or expand their trip to 24, 48, or even all fifty of the United States. Present-day explorers will most likely encounter similar weather to that faced by the earlier explorers, but may find different animals guarding homes—although nothing has ever been a sure thing in the new land Tocqueville experienced.

Tocqueville and Beaumont covered 7,384 miles (not including their side excursions) mostly by foot, horseback, steamboats and stagecoaches. Their American travels came after their 3,356-mile trip across the Atlantic to reach America. In 1832, they set sail again retracing those miles in order to return to their beloved France. Tourists today have the choice of using more modern modes of transportation, or availing themselves of similar conveyances as the French visitors did in 1831–32. For example, steamboats still ply the Mississippi River as they did when Andrew Jackson was President. When Jackson was President in 1830, the United States had 12,866,020 residents in an expanding country. As the nation counts down to the year 2000 the population now approaches 300 million with its frontiers already stretched, and its land increasingly filled.

Alexis de Tocqueville was an aristocrat, a fact of which he was well aware. He was born in Paris to a noble family on July 29, 1805 and died on April 16, 1859 in Cannes, France. He was buried on May 10, 1859 in a cemetery abutting the village of Tocqueville's Roman Catholic church.

In the United States, Alexis de Tocqueville had seen the irresistible future heading toward Europe as the inexorable and unyielding democratic spirit and style spread. Readers of this book can also explore America's future through examining its past as the twenty-first century opens to the continuing American saga. As Tocqueville had realized in February 1832, after spending less than 10 months in America, his quest to understand democracy in America had just started. It would take him two volumes and almost a decade to finish his work. Indeed, as you open the pages of this book, your adventure in following Tocqueville and Beaumont's steps has just begun. The journey to understand and explore American democracy and its republican government continues; your trip will be in the democratic tradition recounted in the pages of *Democracy in America*.

John Splaine
University of Maryland
College Park, Maryland
March 1998

Preface

The original inspiration for *Traveling Tocqueville's America* came in the form of political speeches—hundreds of them.

Since its creation by the cable industry in 1979, C-SPAN has televised American politics in long form. Time and again we've heard political figures—presidents and congressmen, liberals and conservatives—make speeches quoting from Alexis de Tocqueville's classic work *Democracy in America.* Our collective curiosities were aroused and C-SPAN set out to learn more about this 26-year-old French aristocrat and what he had written about 1830s America.

Alexis de Tocqueville and his friend Gustave de Beaumont visited America in 1831–32. Over nine months, the pair visited 17 of the country's then 24 states, with an official mandate from the French government to tour American prisons and write a report on their effectiveness. They visited America's largest cities and traveled to the edges of the frontier, all the while making extensive notes of their observations and conducting many interviews.

Tocqueville returned to France and wrote his prison report, but it was his two-volume treatise, *Democracy in America,* that made him famous. Tocqueville's goal was to understand and report on the roots of American democracy. He surmised that democracy would come to his homeland; as a patriot, he wanted fellow Frenchmen to prepare for the best and worst that democratic forms of government had to offer.

Although it was written in French, *Democracy in America* has had a greater staying power in the United States than in France. The book has never been out of print since the publication of its first volume in 1835. Interested readers can find versions of the book in nearly any American bookstore or library.

After a year of research and planning, C-SPAN was ready in May of 1997 to retrace Tocqueville's nine-month tour. Our goal was to visit each site on the day the Frenchmen had visited more than 150 years earlier. Traveling in a 45-foot, high-tech, yellow bus which served as a network production vehicle, C-SPAN's own 55-stop Tocqueville Tour was transmitted live to the audience of our nationwide public affairs network. For viewers, C-SPAN supported more than 65 hours of programming with annotated route maps, reading materials, an interactive web site and local town hall discussions. Teachers were offered detailed lesson plans and encouraged to use the series video in their classroom.

Nine months is a long run for any television series. Yet, television by its nature is ephemeral. That's why the C-SPAN staffers who were involved with the Tocqueville project decided that something should be done to preserve it for the future. Thus, this tour book came to be.

To mark the route of the two French travelers, each of the 55 cities on the Tocqueville Tour has been presented with a C-SPAN bronze historical plaque. The plaques, together with this book, allow interested tourists to embark on their own version of the Tocqueville tour, absorbing local cultures and history along the way. Whenever available, plaque locations are noted throughout the book.

Every chapter of *Traveling Tocqueville's America* offers a brief synopsis of what Tocqueville and Beaumont found when they visited the site; readers also learn about life in the city today. There is information on local historical offerings and other places of interest. Readers are given contacts for information on local hotels and visitors bureaus. Suggested routes to each stop are also supplied.

Tocqueville and Beaumont's descriptions of the locations they visited introduce many of the chapters. Photographs, historical notes and other illustrations are featured throughout the book. Of special interest may be the historical illustrations—reprints of actual sketches drawn by Gustave de Beaumont, Tocqueville's fellow traveler, as the pair toured the 1830s landscape.

The foreword to this book was written by John Splaine, a professor of education at the University of Maryland. John Splaine, who followed the Tocqueville Tour on his own, served as C-SPAN's chief historical consultant on the project. Nearly all of C-SPAN's 250 staffers were involved in some ways with our Tocqueville project. While it is impossible to name them all, we should tell you about the special efforts of a few.

C-SPAN's Anne Bentzel wrote this book, with editing by Karen Jarmon and Susan Swain; the designer for this book and much of our Tocqueville materials was Margret Lloyd; research for this book was done by Erika Robinson, Ed Aymar and Marybeth Murphy; both Danny Byrd and Barkley Kern handled the business end of the book; staff of the Affiliate Relations unit, which operates the C-SPAN School Buses, planned and carried out all of the 55 stops; Mark Farkas, Kiersten Marshall and Maura Pierce produced much of the Tocqueville programming over the nine months of the tour; and Joanne Wheeler and Kate Mills provided overall direction for the Tocqueville project.

While we're expressing our appreciation, thanks must go to the hundreds of non-C-SPAN people who assisted us in our Tocqueville undertaking. They include Tocqueville's descendants, the family D'Herouville; our team of academic advisors, whose names are listed in the appendix; thousands of teachers who have brought Tocqueville into their college and high school classrooms; the hundreds of people in each of the 55 cities who helped with our research and local production; and, C-SPAN's local cable affiliates who hosted us in the Tocqueville sites and who regularly carry our public affairs programming into American households.

Readers unfamiliar with C-SPAN should know that C-SPAN is unique among television networks. It was created nearly 20 years ago by America's cable television companies to offer non-commercial public affairs programming as a public service. Our operations are supported by their affiliate fees. Today, more than 70 million U.S. households receive C-SPAN. Millions more receive supplemental information about C-SPAN programming from our internet site.

C-SPAN embarked on this historical project to foster a modern-day dialogue on American democracy. It is our hope that readers of this book who embark on historical tours of their own will use it to learn more about the unique history and culture of our nation.

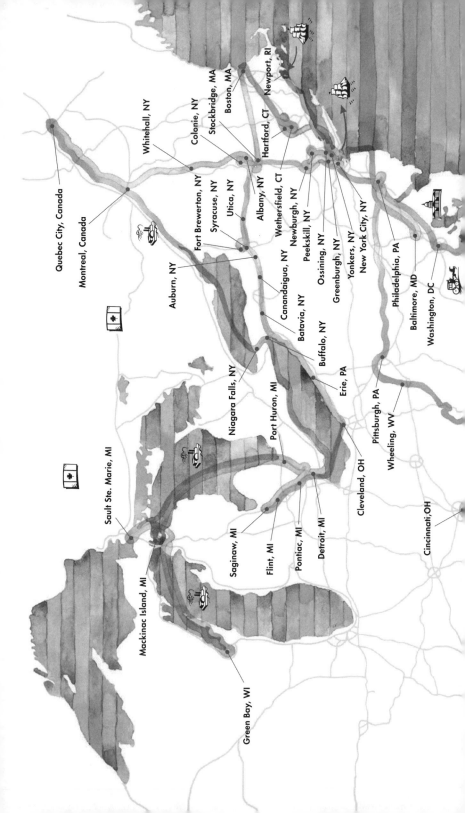

Norfolk, VA

Fayetteville, NC

Columbia, SC

Augusta, GA

Milledgeville, GA

Macon, GA

Westport, KY

Louisville, KY

Knoxville, GA

Nashville, TN

Montgomery, AL

Memphis, TN

Mobile, AL

New Orleans, LA

C-SPAN

Traveling Tocqueville's America

"I confess that in America I saw more than America;
I sought there the image of democracy itself,
with its inclinations, its character, its prejudices,
and its passions,
in order to learn what we have to fear or
to hope from its progress."

—Alexis de Tocqueville, 1835, *Democracy in America*

> *"We went to visit the town, which seemed to us very attractive. It's true we weren't difficult. It's a collection of small houses, the size of chicken coops, but distinguished by a cleanness that is a pleasure to see and that we have no conception of in France."* —Alexis de Tocqueville

Newport
Rhode Island

Tocqueville never planned to go to Newport. Hunger, thirst and a strong wind brought Tocqueville, Beaumont and their fellow passengers from France to the docks of this seaport town. The weary travelers landed there because the captain of the *Havre* had badly mismanaged rations; Tocqueville and his shipmates were starving and desperately in need of fresh water.

At the first sight of land—Newport—the passengers asked the captain to anchor instead of sailing on to New York City. "Never I guess were people so happy to be alive," Tocqueville wrote of his first few minutes on American soil. The famished voyagers walked straight to an inn where the captain treated them to dinner. They returned to the ship that night, and the next day Tocqueville and Beaumont were up with the sun, eager to explore their first American town.

For Tocqueville and his friend Beaumont, who had spent 37 days at sea anxiously awaiting a glimpse of the young nation, the sights of Newport formed their first impressions of the United States. Today Newport, with its

colonial houses, Gilded Age mansions and naval industry, is a thriving town, rich in history. But Newport in 1831 had seen grander days. Unemployment and inflation had followed the Revolutionary War and much of the commerce had moved north to Providence.

When Tocqueville arrived, 60 years before Vanderbilt and other wealthy families built their opulent summer "cottages," Newport was only beginning to stir. One sign of revitalization was the growing number of banks in town. Beaumont counted five; he was amazed that a small town should

At 8:30 on the evening of May 9, Tocqueville and Beaumont first came ashore in America, landing at the Long Wharf area where the Newport Marriott now stands.

Beaumont's drawing of Newport harbor

The Point of Pineapples

Whether they are sculpted from stone or carved in wood, there is no getting past the many pineapples that adorn the houses in this seaport town. The pineapple is a sign of hospitality stemming from colonial times when sailors placed the fruit (generally brought from the West Indies) outside their doors. This showed that the seafarer was home and that guests could stop by and sample the tropical fruit.

possess so many banks.

The number of banks in town confirmed an opinion Beaumont had heard aboard the *Havre*. Peter

Schermerhorn, a wealthy New York businessman and a bank director himself, told Tocqueville and Beaumont that the worst fault of the American character was the overwhelming drive to make money. Beaumont believed him, and wrote that the banks in Newport were evidence that Americans were "entirely commercial."

The two men stayed in Newport for only a short time. In the afternoon of May 10, they boarded a steamship bound for New York City. But their visit to Newport was important. It was their first taste of America, and it formed an impression that never left them.

What to See

The White Horse Tavern

On the corner of Marlborough and Farewell Streets, this award-winning colonial inn may have been the very tavern where Tocqueville, Beaumont and the rest of the hungry passengers of the *Havre* sat down to dinner. What Tocqueville liked best about his meal was the water. Today, the White Horse Tavern boasts a refined menu featuring a fine clam chowder and elegantly prepared fresh seafood.

One of America's oldest taverns, the inn was built before 1673 and served as a meeting place for members of the colony's public officials, many of whom charged their meals to the public treasury. Owners ranged from a pirate to a patriot, but the inn remained in the same family for over 200 years.

In 1776, the owner, Walter Nichols, moved his family and business out of the tavern to avoid living under the same roof as the Hessian mercenaries who stayed at the inn. After the Revolutionary War, he returned and reopened the tavern. 26 Marlborough Street. Tel: (401) 849-3600.

Newport's White Horse Tavern

Trinity Church in Newport

Trinity Church

The architecture of Trinity Church so impressed Beaumont that, not only did he write home about it, he also sketched it. Completed in 1726, the church was designed by Richard Munday. A master builder, Munday was influenced by the English architect Christopher Wren who helped rebuild London from the ashes of the Great Fire of 1666.

Years before Tocqueville landed in Newport, George Washington attended services at Trinity Church. The church contains a rare colonial triple-deck, wine-colored glass pulpit and stained glass by Tiffany and LaFarge. Spring Street, Queen Anne Square.

The Museum of Newport History

In the old Brick Market, located just across from the Old Colony House, is a museum that provides visitors with a good sense of what Newport life was like in years past. With historic photographs, paintings and artifacts of daily life, the museum tells the story of Newport and its people. The museum displays landscapes showing what Newport looked like when Tocqueville visited. To learn more about the Gilded Age, visitors can "board" a reconstructed 1840s omnibus for a film on the development of the mansions. Thames Street. Tel: (401) 841-8770.

Easton's Point

Newport boasts the largest collection of 200-year-old homes in the country, and most stand within a small seven-block area, between Washington Street and Spring Street, called the Point. Beaumont wrote that the houses were so small and perfect they resembled "opera scenery." Thanks to the historic preservation movement which began in the 1960s, more than 90 percent have been restored to their former beauty. **Newport On Foot** offers guided tours of the historic neighborhood. **On Foot** has other tours of Newport, including "Ghost Stories and Graveyards" and "Long Lost Taverns." Tel: (401) 846-5391.

Hunter House

A truly authentic colonial merchant house, this site contains treasures such as a painting by Rhode Island artist Gilbert Stuart and elegant wood furniture crafted by the town's world famous cabinet makers, Townsend and Goddard. This home first galvanized the Newport Preservation Society into action and set the standard for all future restorations. The recently restored colonial garden overlooks Narragansett Bay. 54 Washington Street. Tel: (401) 847-1000.

Touro Synagogue

During Tocqueville's visit, this simple building on Touro Street was only used infrequently for special services. The first synagogue in the country, it is an enduring symbol of Rhode Island's unique beginning.

Roger Williams, the founder of the colony, settled the area with one intent: to provide a place where the government had no power over religion. The trading vessels sailing from Newport spread the news, and soon freedom seekers came to the colony. Among them were the Jews of Spain and Portugal who commissioned Peter Harrison to design a synagogue. Finished in 1763, the simple Georgian exterior belies an ornate interior. Tours are conducted every half hour.
85 Touro Street.
Tel: (401) 847-4794.

Redwood Library and Athenaeum

Tocqueville would have been heartened to know that the Redwood Library existed. He complained that, "one of the drawbacks of American society... is its want of intellectual tone." If Tocqueville had wandered a little further afield, he would have discovered the Redwood Library with its 750 titles. Founded in 1747, it is the oldest continually operating library in the country and holds more than 155,000 volumes. It also houses a special collection of 18th-century English furniture, interior designs, paintings and sculpture.
50 Bellevue Avenue.
Tel: (401) 847-0292.

The Newport Historical Society

The society owns and runs the Museum of Newport History located on Thames Street. The headquarters also features changing exhibits.
82 Touro Street.
Tel: (401) 846-0813.

The Old Colony House

Rhode Island's first government building, it was built in 1739 by master architect Richard Munday. Washington, Jefferson, Lafayette, Jackson and Eisenhower all visited here. The Declaration of Independence was first proclaimed to the citizens of Newport from the 2nd floor balcony. Washington Square.
Tel: (401) 846-0813.

Inns and Outs

How to get there:
From 95 north, take Route 138 east (exit three in Rhode Island) and continue over the Jamestown Bridge and the Newport Bridge. To reach downtown Newport, take the first exit off Newport Bridge (Scenic Newport).

6

Newport's Historic Waterfront

Newport mansion and lighthouse overlooking the harbor

Where to stay:
For information on lodging (which is heavily booked in summer months) and other Newport attractions, contact the Visitor Information Center.
23 America's Cup Avenue, Newport, RI 02840.
Tel: (401) 849-8048, www.gonewport.com.

Newport
Today

More than 28,000 people live in Newport today. Because it's a popular vacation spot, the population triples in the summer months. One of the biggest draws is the annual jazz festival held in Fort Adams State Park in mid-August. Although tourism is Newport's fastest growing industry, the U.S. Navy constitutes a large presence here. Just outside of town is the Naval War College where much of the Persian Gulf War strategy was planned.

Other Attractions

Mansions
No visit to Newport is complete without a look at the extravagant summer homes of the 19th-century elite. The Preservation Society of Newport maintains nine of the estates.
424 Bellevue Avenue.
Tel: (401) 847-1000.

The Cliff Walk
One of the best ways to see the mansions is to walk the 3.5-mile path that snakes along the coast and skirts the backyards of the estates. The walk begins on Memorial Avenue and ends at Bellevue Avenue.

The Museum of Yachting
This museum tells the history of yachting and Newport's harbor.
Fort Adams.
Tel: (401) 847-1018.

Viking Harbor Tours
For a look at Newport from the water, visitors can take a one- or two-hour cruise.
Goat Island Marina.
Tel: (401) 847-6921.

Newport Vineyards and Winery
This is the place to sample some of Newport's own vintage. A short drive from downtown.
909 East Main Road,
(Rte 138) Middletown.
Tel: (401) 848-5161.

> *"...the city is bizarre and not very agreeable. One sees neither dome, nor bell tower, nor great edifice, with the result that one has the constant impression of being in a suburb."*
>
> —Alexis de Tocqueville

New York City
New York

Much has changed in the Big Apple since Tocqueville and Beaumont visited. According to the Frenchmen, the city was rather provincial in 1831. Beaumont described the roads as badly paved, and the fine arts as undeveloped. He considered the museums, which featured stuffed birds and magic lanterns instead of paintings, laughable.

Tocqueville and Beaumont checked into a boarding house at 66 Broadway, the most fashionable street in town, and stayed in the city for two weeks meeting politicians, visiting prisons and mixing with New York society.

The two French nobles were a sensation. News of their arrival hit the streets in the May 12th edition of the *Mercantile Advertiser* and was soon picked up by the *New York Evening Post*. From the governor to the mayor, New Yorkers eagerly vied for a chance to meet them, flattered that two emissaries from the French government wanted to learn about the U.S. prison system.

Official tours of a penitentiary, a mental institute and a poorhouse were quickly organized by the mayor and city alderman.

St. Paul's Church and the Broadway Stages, 1831

8

The Wall in Wall Street

Over three hundred years ago, there really was a wall on Wall Street. Built in 1653 by the Dutch to guard their first settlement, it was a stockade wall made of wood with a deep ditch alongside it. The wall stood until 1699 when the British tore it down.

Tocqueville and Beaumont also managed to enjoy a few social outings. Peter Schermerhorn, who befriended them aboard the *Havre,* was a member of one of the wealthiest merchant families in New York. With Schermerhorn's introductions, Tocqueville and Beaumont attended parties in the gracious summer homes that lined the East River.

Not much of the old New York that Tocqueville and Beaumont described in their letters remains. On a bitter 17-below-zero night in 1835, part of the city was razed by a fire that destroyed 650 buildings. The Bank of New York now towers over the spot where Tocqueville and Beaumont's boarding house stood. A few steps away, Bowling Green, the city's first park, still exists.

On weekdays, lower Broadway bustles with the activity that impressed Tocqueville; even in 1831, New York hummed with commerce. It was already the largest city in the nation and growing rapidly.

Tocqueville felt that the freedom Americans enjoyed might be the source of the New Yorkers' energy. He wrote, "Here freedom is unrestrained, and subsists by being useful to every one without injuring anybody. There is something undeniably feverish in the activity it imparts to industry and to the human spirit."

What to See

South Street Seaport Museum

When Peter Schermerhorn purchased this lot in the 1790s, it was all water. Schermerhorn quickly filled it in and built the block of buildings that became the heart of New York's shipping world.

Today this 11-square-block area of cobblestone streets and historic buildings is a living museum, telling the story of the city's waterways, complete with galleries, restaurants and shops. Schermerhorn Row is the oldest surviving row of buildings in the city. On weekends, street musicians and artists perform in the adjacent square.

A walk toward the river leads you to the six historic ships dating from 1885 to 1930 that are docked at the piers. The fleet is open for tours and some cruises. South Street Seaport also has a children's center and several galleries. For fresh fish, visit the Fulton Fish Market at the end of Fulton Street.

For tickets and more information, go to the Visitors Center at 12 Fulton Street. Tel: (212) 748-8600.

Trinity Church

The spires of Trinity Church stand majestically amidst the

To learn more about publishing in the 1800s, stop by Bowne & Co., Stationers, located in the South Street Seaport at 211 Water Street. It is an operating 19th-century printing shop.

New York City, NY

9

New York City, New York

Lower Manhattan

skyscrapers of Wall Street. The congregation has been here since 1696. Trinity Church that now stands on the corner of Broadway and Wall Street is not the same building that Tocqueville and Beaumont saw. That church was later deemed unsafe and subsequently torn down.

The current church was built in 1846. It contains a small museum which is open daily. A walk through the burial grounds leads you to a number of interesting tombstones, including that of Alexander Hamilton. Trinity Church also offers a noonday concert series.
Tel: (212) 602-0872 for museum, (212) 602-0768 for concert information.

A walk through New York City's financial district still offers a hint of yesteryear. The narrow, winding streets and their old-fashioned names, such as Maiden Lane, Water Street and Front Street, evoke earlier times.

The Museum of the City of New York

This dream-come-true museum is perfect for history buffs. Established in 1923, the Museum of the City of New York tells the story of the Big Apple. Visitors can find everything from historical prints and early photographs of life in the city to elaborate, antique doll houses. The museum contains antique clothing, decorative arts, prints and photographs, paintings, sculptures, toys and a theater collection featuring costume and set designs from big-name musicals. In the fall and spring, the museum offers historical walking tours of New York City.
1220 Fifth Avenue at 103rd Street. Tel: (212) 534-1672.

Snug Harbor Cultural Center

Situated on Staten Island, Snug Harbor was built in 1801 as a home and hospital for retired sailors. The iron fence surrounding the grounds was intended to keep the sailors on the island and away from the temptation of New York City's seaport taverns. Snug Harbor sprawls over 83 green acres of park land and provides space for modern art, theater and outdoor concerts. The Staten Island Children's Museum is located on the grounds, as are other museums. Look for signs to the Visitors Center.
1000 Richmond Terrace. Tel: (718) 448-2500.

10

Historic Richmond Town
Staten Island's historic museum town features 27 reconstructed 17th-, 18th- and 19th-century buildings. The "town" sprawls over 100 acres; here you'll find the oldest elementary school in the nation. Costumed guides tell the stories of historic Staten Island. 441 Clarke Avenue. Tel: (718) 351-1611.

The New York Historical Society
The city's oldest museum, the New York Historical Society, has an impressive collection of six million pieces of art, literature and memorabilia documenting New York City life. Tocqueville arrived just as American painting was beginning to flourish. During the 1830s, Luman Reed, a wealthy city merchant, was busy collecting the latest American art. Today, the Historical Society houses the Luman Reed Collection, including Thomas Cole's magnificent series of paintings. 170 Central Park West. Tel: (212) 873-3400.

Battery Park
At the southernmost tip of Manhattan, Battery Park is one of the few places in the city that Tocqueville might still recognize. One dramatic difference is Castle Clinton. The large circular stone structure that dominates the park was an island during Tocqueville's visit. Visitors reached the castle, which served as an amphitheater, by crossing a drawbridge. Later, landfill was added, and Castle Clinton became part of Battery Park. Today you can buy tickets in the Castle for Ellis Island and the Statue of Liberty. Named for the British gun battery that was housed there from 1683 to 1687, the park offers spectacular views of Lady Liberty, Ellis Island and the New Jersey shoreline.

Merchant's House Museum
Located in what would have been the New York City suburbs of 1831, the Merchant's House Museum is the perfectly preserved 19th-century home of the Tredwell family. Seabury Tredwell was a wealthy merchant who owned a shop on downtown Pearl Street. He built his house in 1832, far from the bustle of the city. If he had wanted, Tredwell could have used New York's first commuter transportation, a horse-drawn omnibus, to get to work. The journey would have taken about 40 minutes. Today the house contains furniture, clothing and family memorabilia. 29 East Fourth Street. Tel: (212) 777-1089.

City Hall
Built in 1803, City Hall has served as the center for the city's administration since the start of the 19th century. Tocqueville may have entered the ornate building during his meetings with the mayor or city officials, or could have wandered through City Hall Park which has been a public place since 1686. These green lawns and bright gardens are the same place where public executions once occurred. Along with the mayor's offices, City Hall contains the Governor's Room and George Washington's writing desk. In April 1865, Abraham Lincoln's body lay in state at the head of the staircase. Broadway and Murray Street. Tel: (212) 566-5250.

New York City skyline

Fraunces Tavern Museum

Washington said farewell to his officers at the end of the Revolutionary War in the tavern's Long Room. When Tocqueville arrived in New York City, the tavern, located close to the seaport, was a boarding house of rather dubious nature. It was restored and opened to the public in 1907. Today the tavern serves lunch and dinner. The museum upstairs showcases a re-creation of an 18th-century public tavern and a 19th-century private dining room.
54 Pearl Street.
Tel: (212) 425-1778.

New York City
Today

In New York City you can find almost everything. With over seven million residents, New York is the largest city in the nation and one of the financial, entertainment and publishing capitals of the world. In addition to a variety of museums, shops and theaters, the city offers a host of ethnic celebrations throughout the year.

Inns and Outs

How to get there:

To reach midtown Manhattan from the south, take the New Jersey Turnpike (I-95) to the Lincoln Tunnel (exit 16E). From New England, take I-95 to the Triboro Bridge and continue onto FDR Drive, which runs along the east side of Manhattan and exits onto city streets.

Where to stay:

For information on lodging in the city, contact the New York City Visitors Hotel Hotline

Metropolitan Museum of Art

12

at (800) 846-7666.
For events and attractions,
contact the New York
Convention and Visitors Bureau.
810 Seventh Avenue 3rd floor,
New York, NY 10019.
Tel: (212) 397-8200.
www.nycvisit.com

Other Attractions

Empire State Building
One of the world's tallest
buildings, this famous New York
skyscraper has an observatory
tower which looks out on a
50-mile view of the city.
350 Fifth Avenue at 34th Street.
Tel: (212) 736-3100.

Metropolitan Museum of Art
The Metropolitan is home to
both traveling and permanent
exhibits including Egyptian,
European, African and
Medieval art, sculptures, photos
and costumes.
1000 Fifth Avenue
at 82nd Street.
Tel: (212) 535-7710.

Rockefeller Center
Stretching over 22
acres of Manhattan,
this business and
entertainment
center houses
numerous
underground shops
and restaurants. A
sunken plaza
features ice skating
in the winter and a
café during the
spring and summer.
Fifth Avenue

and 8th Street.
Tel: (212) 698-2950.

Ellis Island and the Statue of Liberty
Take the South Ferry from the
city to see New York's most
famous symbol of freedom,
Lady Liberty. Nearby is Ellis
Island which includes the
American Immigrant Wall of
Honor, the Immigration Library,
and exhibits chronicling the
historic entry point to America
for millions of immigrants.
Tel: (212) 363-3200.

Lincoln Center for the Performing Arts
Seven performance facilities
comprise the cultural hub of
New York City which stretches
over several blocks of upper
Manhattan. Lincoln Square is
located at the intersection of
Broadway and Columbus
Avenue on 66th Street.
Tel: (212) 870-1630.

Statue of Liberty

> *"There is no more delicious sight than the spectacle offered by its banks. There reigns an air of prosperity, activity and industry that rejoices the sight."*
>
> —Alexis de Tocqueville

Ossining
New York

Here on the banks of the Hudson River lies Sing Sing, one of America's most famous prisons. The expression "being sent up the river" originated here because many convicts were sent from New York City via the Hudson River north to Sing Sing. A total of 614 people have been electrocuted at the penitentiary including Julius and Ethel Rosenberg, executed for espionage in 1953. The prison has been operating since 1825 and is still in use today, but is not open to the public.

In 1831 when Tocqueville and Beaumont arrived to study the prison, they observed 30 guards ruling over 900 silent inmates. Control was enforced by harsh punishment. "One cannot see the prison of Sing Sing and the system of labour which is there established without being struck by astonishment and fear," wrote Tocqueville. The two men spent nine days interviewing guards and collecting statistics.

Despite the long afternoons spent in the grim confines of the penitentiary, Tocqueville and Beaumont found peace, relaxation and even time for profound thinking in this small river town. In the evening, they swam in the river and socialized. Ossining was impressed with the two young men. *The Westchester Herald* described them as "gentlemen of engaging manners, of first rate talents."

In Ossining, during a Sunday service at Sing Sing prison, Beaumont witnessed the country's religious tolerance. And it is in Ossining that Tocqueville wrote down the true mission of his journey, "... to know the country we are traveling through. To succeed in that, we are obliged to decompose society... and search out the elements of which it is composed at home, in order to be able to ask useful questions and forget nothing here."

For a panoramic view of the river, one that mirrors Beaumont's sketches, go to the Louis Engle Park at the foot of Sing Sing prison on Westerly Road. Look for the C-SPAN plaque on the replica of the prison guards' tower.

14   Sing Sing prison

What's in a name?

That is a question local residents have asked for a century. Incorporated into Westchester County in 1813, the village of Sing Sing got its name from the Sint-Sinck Indians who once lived here. But in 1902, a group of village council men, unhappy with the town's association with the prison, voted to change the name to Ossining. The name won by one vote; the runner-up was Weskora, after an Indian chief. Not to be outdone, the prison changed its name in 1970 to Ossining Correctional Facility, but later changed it back to Sing Sing Correctional Facility.

What to See

Teatown Lake Reservation

Spanning 730 acres, this education center and nature preserve offers natural history exhibits, seasonal programs for adults and children and more than 12 miles of hiking trails. Teatown hosts tours of Wildflower Island, a habitat which is adorned with colorful fields of wildflowers. Guided excursions to the island are offered from mid-April to September. 1600 Spring Valley Road. Tel: (914) 762-2912.

Ossining Urban Cultural Park & Joseph G. Caputo Community Center

This museum, also known as the Ossining Visitors Center, provides an interesting overview of Sing Sing prison history. Replicas of an electric chair, a prison cell circa 1800 and anecdotes about Sing Sing wardens create a sense of the penitentiary's past.

The center also houses exhibits about the Old Croton Aqueduct, built in 1837 to bring fresh water to New York City. A precarious feat, the construction of the aqueduct caused so many deaths that a large number of widows were forced to work. As a result, the town started one of the first child care centers in the country. 95 Broadway. Tel: (914) 941-3189.

Ossining Historical Society

In this charming old house, visitors can find everything from hat boxes and Indian artifacts to family bibles. The Historical Society features exhibits on the history of Sing Sing prison and displays portraits of early residents. A Victorian doll house and antique toys are located on the second floor. The museum also contains a thrift shop and a library containing over 1,000 volumes. 196 Croton Avenue. Tel: (914) 941-0001.

Ossining Today

The city's population is more than 20,000. Although the prison still provides many jobs for residents of Ossining, most people commute to nearby White Plains or New York City. Town officials are working to develop additional tourism projects connected with the prison.

Crowds enjoy a summer festival

15

Inns and Outs

How to get there:

From New York City take I-95 east (US 1) to I-87 and head north for 17 miles. Take a right at US 202 (US 9) and drive 6 miles to Ossining, New York.

From New Jersey take Highway 9 heading northeast for 12 miles. Turn left on Highway 87 for 17 miles. Take a right on US 202 (US 9) and drive 6 miles to Ossining, New York.

Where to stay:

For lodging information, contact the Greater Ossining Chamber of Commerce. PO Box 382, Ossining, NY 10562. Tel: (914) 941-0009. Also try the Tarrytown Chamber of Commerce. 54 Main Street, Tarrytown, NY 10591. Tel: (914) 631-1705.

The house where Tocqueville and Beaumont boarded stands on 34 State Street. Now a privately owned wood-working company, the house gained additions and levels since 1831. It is made of Sing Sing marble, which is actually a pale limestone that was quarried by prison inmates.

Other Attractions

Old Croton Trailway State Park

For a scenic view of the historic towns along the Hudson, visitors can take a walk along the aqueduct trailway. The trail starts at Yonkers and goes to Croton Gorge Park where a waterfall and picnic area provide a comfortable stop. The trail hits Ossining on Main Street and continues on through the downtown area. 15 Walnut Street, Dobbs Ferry. Tel: (914) 693-5259. Tours of the aqueduct are available by appointment. Tel: (914) 941-3189.

The Old Dutch Church and Cemetery of Sleepy Hollow

The cemetery of Sleepy Hollow, where Washington Irving's headless horseman galloped, is located just a few miles south of Ossining. (Take Rt. 9 to Tarrytown.) Eleanor Van Tassel Brush, a probable model for Katrina in *The Legend of Sleepy Hollow,* is buried here as is Irving himself. Washington Irving's grave is situated on a hill in the modern part of the cemetery which overlooks the old Dutch burial grounds. The 300-year-old church is one of the oldest in America. Tours of the church and the grounds take place from Memorial Day through the end of October. 430 North Broadway, Sleepy Hollow. Tel: (914) 631-1123.

16   34 State Street

Greenburgh
New York

In 1831, the town of Greenburgh was mostly rolling farmland. Not too far from the feverish pace of New York City, it was a popular spot to build summer homes. Many of these 17th-century summer escapes still dot the banks of the Hudson River. The Hudson Valley, of which Greenburgh is a part, has the largest concentration of historic sites in the nation.

The Livingston family, who had met Tocqueville and Beaumont in New York City, owned a summer house in Greenburgh. The family invited the Frenchmen to its summer estate for an elaborate dinner, but Tocqueville and Beaumont never made it. Something must have gotten lost in the translation; on the day of the affair, Tocqueville and Beaumont sat quietly in their nearby boarding house, completely unaware that a party was being thrown in their honor.

A few days later, Tocqueville and Beaumont came to Greenburgh to make amends. They arrived at three o'clock on June 7th, just as the Livingston family was sitting down to dinner. Their visit was one Tocqueville would remember.

During the course of their conversation, Mr. Livingston brought up a topic that was of great interest to any aristocrat— inheritance laws. Tocqueville wondered how these inheritance laws, which he perceived as being based more on equality than on tradition, affected family wealth.

Months later he penned his thoughts in *Democracy in America*. "It is not then by interest, but by common associations and by the free sympathy of opinion and of taste, that democracy unites brothers to each other. It divides their inheritance, but allows their hearts and minds to unite."

The C-SPAN plaque, marking Tocqueville's travels, is located at the Greenburgh Town Hall. 320 Tarrytown Road, Elmsford, NY.

The Hudson River Valley

Cock "Tales" Anyone?

Legend has it that the cocktail got its name in Elmsford, one of the small villages that makes up Greenburgh. During the American Revolution, a barmaid, unable to find a spoon to stir a drink, plucked a feather from a nearby rooster. All night long, she mixed drinks with the cock's feather, and thus the cocktail found its name.

What to See

Sunnyside Manor

Washington Irving, author of *Rip Van Winkle* and *The Legend of Sleepy Hollow,* bought this

Irving's study at Sunnyside Manor

small farm house in 1835. He named it the "snuggery" and remodeled it, creating a charming cottage straight from his tales of Knickerbocker New York. Today, costumed guides lead visitors through the grounds and a house filled with Irving's memorabilia. West Sunnyside Lane, Tarrytown.
Tel: (914) 631-8702 or (800) 448-4007.

Rudy's Beau Rivage Restaurant

This bright red restaurant serves Italian food and is a frequent site for wedding receptions. Historians believe it was owned by the Livingston family. Despite some modern additions to the house, there are still some traces of the original elegant architecture. The view of the Hudson from the back patio is spectacular. Located off Rt. 9 on 19 Livingston Avenue in Dobbs Ferry.
Tel: (914) 693-3192.

Lyndhurst

Railroad magnate Jay Gould owned this opulent Gothic-style mansion, overlooking the Hudson River. He commuted to his job on Wall Street via his private yacht. Built in 1838 by Alexander Jackson Davis, the house contains a collection of 19th- and 20th-century art, elegant gardens and a coachhouse restaurant.
635 South Broadway, Tarrytown.
Tel: (914) 631-4481.

Inns and Outs

How to get there:
Greenburgh is located just north of New York City. Follow I-95 to I-87 north, continue on I-87 to I-287 east. Follow I-287 east to Sprain Brook Parkway. The parkway leads into the Greenburgh exit at Central Avenue.

18 Sunnyside, home of Washington Irving

Marc Chagall stained-glass window in Union Church of Pocantico

Where to stay:
For suggestions on where to stay, contact the Westchester Convention and Visitors Bureau. 235 Mamaroneck Avenue, White Plains, NY 10605. Tel: (914) 948-0047 or (800) 833-WCVB.

Greenburgh
Today

Greenburgh is located in the lower central part of Westchester County and is part of the Hudson River Valley. It is made up of six small unincorporated villages, including Ardsley, Dobbs Ferry, Elmsford, Hastings-on-Hudson, Irvington and Tarrytown. The population is approximately 80,000.

Other
Attractions
Van Cortlandt Manor
Overlooking the Hudson and Croton Rivers, this 18th-century mansion was home to one of New York's most influential families. The manor has gardens and craft demonstrations and features Georgian and Federal furnishings. Look for the

18th-century tavern, located on the grounds. It once served as lodging for travelers along the Albany Post Road.
South Riverside Avenue, Croton-on-Hudson.
Tel: (914) 271-8981.

Kykuit
One of the Rockefellers' homesteads, this spectacular mansion is located along the Hudson and features beautifully landscaped gardens, vintage automobiles and carriages and a collection of 20th-century sculpture, including works by Pablo Picasso and Henry Moore. Tours by appointment only. Closed from November to May. Pocantico Hills.
Tel: (914) 631-9491 or (914) 631-8200.

Union Church of Pocantico Hills
This delightful country church features stained-glass windows created by artists Marc Chagall and Henri Matisse. The windows are the last work created by Matisse; he died two days after they were finished. Closed January to March.
Pocantico Hills, near Kykuit.
Tel: (914) 631-2069 or (914) 631-8200.

East facade of Kykuit, the Rockefeller Estate

Yonkers
New York

Tocqueville and Beaumont sailed into Yonkers on a sloop. It took two to three hours of what Beaumont called, "delightful sailing" on the single-mast sailboat to reach the village from New York City. They were headed north to Albany and then to points west, but first they wanted to pay a visit to the Livingston family who lived in nearby Greenburgh.

When the Frenchmen arrived, however, the Livingston family was not home. Unable to find a boat to take them up river, Tocqueville and Beaumont whiled away the rest of the warm summer day in Yonkers.

In 1831, Yonkers was a sleepy village surrounded by acres of farmland. The Hudson River Railroad which helped usher the town into the industrial age would not be completed until 1849. Tocqueville took advantage of the pastoral setting to go bird hunting. Beaumont sat by the river to sketch the glorious view of the Hudson. At sunset, the Frenchmen went for a swim in the river and settled in for the night at a local tavern.

Visiting Yonkers today, it is hard to imagine the pastoral scene Beaumont described in a letter to his brother. Now just a short drive from New York City, Yonkers is the fourth largest city in the state. The railroad, the river,

> Look for the C-SPAN plaque, which marks Tocqueville's journey, at the Old Yonkers Pier off Buena Vista Avenue at the end of Main Street.

Beaumont's sketch of Yonkers' pier

20

In a Pickle

In the 1830s, when Tocqueville visited, Yonkers had the handle on the pickle market. Area farmers devoted many of their acres to growing cucumbers for pickling. The town became the chief supplier of pickles for New York State. Yonkers' port became known as the pickle port.

and the town's proximity to New York City have all contributed to making Yonkers an industrial town. The 4 1/2-mile riverfront, along the Hudson, is still the town's prime attraction. From the old steamboat pier, built in 1900, located off Buena Vista Avenue, you can view the New York skyline. Across the river, the high cliffs of New Jersey known as the Palisades tower above the Hudson River.

What to *See*

Hudson River Museum of Westchester

Housed in the opulent Glenview Mansion, the museum reflects the social and artistic history of Yonkers and the Hudson River Valley. Built as a summer house in 1876 by John Bond Trevor, a wealthy New York City financier, the mansion is a rare example of a short-lived Victorian architectural style called Eastlake. The museum contains a planetarium and a collection of Hudson River landscapes.
511 Warburton Avenue.
Tel: (914) 963-4550.

Philipse Manor Hall Historic Site

Situated in downtown Larkin Plaza, Philipse Manor Hall is a testament to the time when manor estates ruled the countryside. When Tocqueville visited, the Manor Hall was a privately owned house. Constructed in the 1680s, the Manor is one of the oldest buildings in Westchester County. The estate was owned by the Philipse family—famous for its support of the British crown. Frederick Philipse, the last owner of the Hall, chose the losing side in the Revolutionary War and was sentenced to death. He wisely emigrated to England and the manor was turned over to the colonial government. Today the house is a museum of area history, art and architecture.
Warburton Avenue and Dock Street.
Tel: (914) 965-4027.

St. John's Episcopal Church

This famous church was under major renovation when Tocqueville and Beaumont visited Yonkers. One of the state's oldest stone churches, it served as a hospital during the Revolutionary War. The church contains some of the first stained glass made in America.
One Hudson Street.
Tel: (914) 963-3033.

Yonkers *Today*

Yonkers has a culturally diverse population of about 200,000 residents and is an active commercial and industrial center.

21

Inns *and* Outs

How to get there:
From New York City, take I-95 north to the George Washington Bridge. Exit the bridge at I-87 north and follow to Yonkers.

Where to stay:
For information on lodging, contact the Westchester Convention and Visitors Bureau. 235 Mamaroneck Avenue, White Plains, NY 10605. Tel: (914) 948-0047 or (800) 833-WCVB.

Tocqueville and Beaumont most likely stayed at the Indian Queen Tavern, the town's most important inn at the time. The tavern, which has been razed, stood on the corner of South Broadway and New Main Street in Getty Square.

Other Attractions

Untermyer Park
A Grecian temple, sculptures by Paul Manship and elegant gardens with a Beaux Arts-style landscape are all located in the park which offers panoramic views of the Hudson River. Isadora Duncan once danced in the gardens.

945 North Broadway. Tel: (914) 377-6442.

St. Paul's Church
Located 10 miles away from Yonkers, St. Paul's Church has a long history. It served as a hospital during the Revolutionary War, a town meeting place and a courtroom. Aaron Burr once worked on cases here. Take the Hutchinson River Parkway, exit 8. 897 South Columbus Avenue, Mount Vernon. Tel: (914) 667-4116.

Yonkers Raceway
Dating back to 1899, the track features year-round nighttime harness racing and daytime simulcasts of the New York Racing Association. Central Park and Yonkers Avenue. Tel: (914) 968-4200.

Yonkers Railroad Station
Designed by Warren & Wetmore in the Beaux Arts style, it is the third railroad station to stand in the location since the Hudson River Railroad opened in 1849. Larkin Plaza and Buena Vista Avenue.

The Indian Queen Tavern

> *"We took a charming promenade through woods and over rocks; and we sweat blood and water to get to the summit of a very high mountain from the top of which we saw one of the most beautiful spectacles and one of the most imposing tableaus that the North River (the Hudson) presents."*
> —Gustave de Beaumont

Peekskill, Bear Mountain & Newburgh
New York

July 1, 1831 was an adventurous day for Tocqueville and Beaumont. They climbed a mountain, raced a steamboat in the middle of the night and watched a display of fireworks explode over the Hudson River. The day began with a steamboat trip from Yonkers to a small village called Caldwell's Landing, located directly across the river from Peekskill. The village of Caldwell no longer exists and the area, now called Jones Point, is part of the town of Stonybrook, New York.

The Frenchmen planned to catch a steamboat later that day and visit West Point. While waiting, Tocqueville and Beaumont climbed the steep banks to see the Hudson. The view they most likely saw was from what today is Bear Mountain State Park; the park still provides spectacular panoramas of the area.

At nine o'clock that night, the steamboat *North America* arrived at the landing, but did not stop. A little boat brought Tocqueville and Beaumont out to the *North America*. A few miles upriver, they passed by Newburgh; skyrockets went off and the horizon exploded with light. The two travelers learned later that the fireworks marked the start of a race between the *North America* and another steamship.

Tocqueville and Beaumont never recorded whether the *North America* won the race. Perhaps they did not care, for, due to the race, the captain refused to stop at West Point. The Frenchmen were disappointed to have missed a visit to America's renowned military academy.

> "All this happened so quickly, in such darkness and on such a vast sheet of water that there was something magical in our taking off," Beaumont wrote upon embarking the *North America*.

Peekskill along the Hudson, 1830.

23

Are You Kidding?

There are many legends of lost treasures in the Hudson River and Highlands. In 1844, just a decade after Tocqueville visited Caldwell's Landing, the Kidd Salvage Company came to Caldwell's Landing to search for buried treasure. The company had heard rumors that Captain Kidd's pirate ship had gone down close to the landing. The Salvage Company gave up after searching for four years and finding nothing but a few rusty ship cannons. The legends still inspire treasure hunters. Nearby Bear Mountain State Park still fields requests from companies interested in searching for lost bounty.

Winner Takes All

Steamboat racing was fairly common in 1831. The faster the steamboat, the more customers it attracted and the higher the fares could be charged. However, passengers were not always told their ship was involved in a race. Fatal accidents were not infrequent and in 1852 the state of New York finally outlawed steamboat racing.

What to *See*

Bear Mountain State Park
Located about ten minutes from Peekskill, this historic park makes up part of the Hudson Highlands. Its name comes from the mountain's shape, said to resemble a sleeping bear. From its summit, you can see the Bear Mountain Bridge, site of a huge iron chain that stretched across the river in 1776. Colonial forces built the chain in a successful effort to prevent British ships from reaching the upper regions of the Hudson. The park offers seasonal swimming, hiking, nature trails, trailside museums and a wildlife center. Located at the intersection of Palisades Parkway and Route 9W. Tel: (914) 786-2701 for general information; (914) 786-2731 for camping and dining information.

West Point
The United States Military Academy at West Point has been the training ground of some of the greatest U.S. officers. Robert E. Lee, Ulysses S. Grant, Douglas MacArthur and Dwight D. Eisenhower are among the luminaries who graduated from the academy which is just a short drive from Newburgh. The academy includes the **West Point Museum** which houses exhibits on weapons and war history and features everything from Napoleon's sword to the safety plug pulled from the atomic bomb dropped on Nagasaki. U.S. Military Academy, Building 2110, West Point. Tel: (914) 938-2203 or (914) 938-4011. **The West Point Cemetery** overlooks the Hudson and, for more than a century, has served as a military burial ground.

Peekskill
Across the river from Bear Mountain lies the historic town of Peekskill. In colonial times, the town was a hub for Washington's forces. Peekskill was attacked and burned twice by the British. While in Peekskill,

The Riverfront Green on Railroad Avenue, which served as the town's former steamboat landing, offers splendid views of the Hudson. Look for the C-SPAN plaque, marking Tocqueville's visit.

24

Hudson River

Benedict Arnold received command of West Point. By 1831, Peekskill was a village of a little over 1,000 people. Steamboats traveling up and down the river stopped there, transporting produce and passengers.

Today Peekskill has made a name for itself as an artists' retreat, providing homes, galleries and studios to over 70 artists. You may want to visit the **Peekskill Downtown Artist Community** for a tour of artists' studios, open every third Saturday of the month. For more information, contact the Peekskill Chamber of Commerce. Tel: (914) 737-3600. The **Peekskill Museum** chronicles the town's history and includes period clothing, furniture and iron stoves for which Peekskill is famous. 124 Union Avenue.
Tel: (914) 736-0473.

Newburgh

As they raced past on the *North America*, Tocqueville and Beaumont saw Newburgh illuminated only by fireworks. They might have spied the **Crawford House**, which lies on a bluff high above the Hudson and offers an unobstructed view of the river. The house, home to Newburgh's historic society, is open on weekends for tours. Exhibits include sloop and steamboat models and empire furniture. 189 Montgomery Street. Tel: (914) 561-2585.

In the 1830s, Newburgh, with its deep water port, was a bustling river town. Area farms provided abundant produce which was shipped to New York City. Shipping brought prosperity into the city and with it a demand for gracious homes. Andrew Jackson Downing, a native of Newburgh, answered the call. He became a leading landscape gardener, architect and horticulturist, designing many of the elegant homes in the town's east end. Downing also contributed to the planning of the Smithsonian Museum and U.S. Capitol grounds. He died in a steamboat accident in 1852. **Andrew Jackson Downing Park** is situated on Robinson Avenue and South Street and provides great views of the Hudson.

Like Peekskill, Newburgh has a rich colonial past. In the final days of the Revolutionary War, Washington made his headquarters in the Hasbrouck House. Here Washington ordered the cease fire that brought the war to a close. Here he also quelled the notion among supporters that he be crowned America's king. **Washington's Headquarters** with its museum and furnished home provides a

look at Revolutionary War times. Look for a portion of the huge chain that stretched across the Hudson to prevent British warships from sailing up river. Open mid-April through October.
84 Liberty Street, Newburgh.
Tel: (914) 562-1195.

Look for the C-SPAN plaque on Newburgh Landing, along Newburgh's historic waterfront.

The Area
Today

Peekskill has a population of about 20,000. The town has done much in recent years to revitalize itself, such as establishing Peekskill's artist community.

Newburgh, primarily a bedroom community of New York City and White Plains, is beginning to capitalize on its picturesque location and historic significance. The town has a population of more than 26,000.

Inns *and* Outs

How to get there:
To get to Peekskill from New York City, take I-95 north to I-87 north. Follow I-87 for 17 miles and turn left on US Highway 202 (US 9) towards Peekskill.

To get to Bear Mountain, take the Palisades Parkway to the intersection of the parkway and Route 9W.

To get to Newburgh from New York City, take the Palisades Parkway north to Route 9W. Head north to Newburgh or take the New York State Thruway to exit 17.

Where to stay:
For lodging in the **Newburgh** area call the Orange County Tourism Center.
40 Matthews Street, Suite 103, Goshen, NY 10924.
(914) 294-8080.

For places to stay in **Peekskill** contact the Peekskill/Cortland Chamber of Commerce.
1 South Division Street, Peekskill, NY 10566.
Tel: (914) 737-3600.

Other Attractions

Hudson Maritime Museum
Farther upriver, the Hudson Maritime Museum takes a look at the history of shipping on the Hudson. Located at Rondout Waterfront, the museum is home to historic vessels. The exhibit hall contains photographs and artifacts from sunken boats and century-old steamboats. The museum also offers a boat ride to visit Rondout Lighthouse, the last Hudson River lighthouse.
One Rondout Landing, Kingston.
Tel: (914) 338-0071.

26   NY Waterway Ferry

"…you see carried in great pomp an old American flag, bullet torn, which has come down from the war of independence. There, in a carriage at the head of the procession, are 3 or 4 old soldiers, who fought with Washington, whom the city preserves like precious relics…"

—Gustave de Beaumont

Albany & Colonie
New York

The two travelers arrived in the state capital on July 2, 1831. Albany, located at the juncture of the Hudson River and the Erie Canal, was a focal point of government and commerce. At the head of State Street, now the Capitol Hill area, government offices clustered around the old Capitol.

Tocqueville and Beaumont were in town to learn about state government. Although the Frenchmen talked to Albany politicians, including the governor, they discovered little about the role state government played in the lives of Americans. Tocqueville wrote, "All the bureaus as all the registers were opened to us, but, as for the Government, we are still seeking it."

From his time in Albany, Tocqueville deduced that state government played a minor

> While in town, Tocqueville and Beaumont stayed at the Eagle Tavern which stood on Court Street, now Broadway.

State Street, 1848

The Greatest Show in Albany

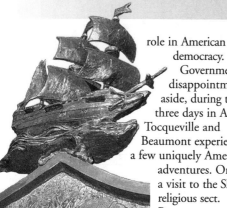

Henry Hudson's
Half Moon weathervane
on top of Albany's
D&H Railroad Building

role in American democracy.

Governmental disappointment aside, during their three days in Albany, Tocqueville and Beaumont experienced a few uniquely American adventures. One was a visit to the Shaker religious sect. Beaumont was especially curious to see the "Quakers Shakers" as he called them. The Shakers are known for their furniture, industriousness, religious dancing and celibacy. On July 3, Tocqueville and Beaumont traveled 12 miles outside of town, to a densely-wooded area now known as Colonie, NY, to watch a Shaker Sunday service.

There they watched men and women form single lines in a large meeting house and hop about like "trained dogs." Tocqueville wrote, "...they (the dancing Shakers) intoned an air more lamentable than all the others, and began to turn about the room, an exercise which they continued during a good quarter hour." The Shakers bewildered the two travelers, but might well have helped reinforce their understanding of America's religious tolerance. Today, you can still visit Colonie and learn about the Shakers' life.

The next morning, Tocqueville and Beaumont awoke to the sounds of a gunfire salute and the ringing of church bells. The Fourth of July celebration had begun. City streets were decked with flags and clogged with people. Soon after breakfast, the Secretary of State and the Lieutenant Governor arrived at their hotel and asked the two French visitors to march with other dignitaries at the head of the Independence Day parade. The parade made its way down Ferry, South and North Pearl Streets, passing by the Old Albany Academy which is now the Joseph Henry Memorial, Albany's oldest civic building and Herman Melville's alma mater.

After the parade, Tocqueville and Beaumont attended a reading of the Declaration of Independence which deeply moved them. The reading was followed by a young lawyer who read a poem that Tocqueville described as "a long rhetorical harangue, in which he pompously passed the entire universe in review to get to the United States, which in all respects, he made the centre of the world."

This deeply upset the French noble and, as he left the church where the reading was held, he was "cursing the orator whose flow of words and stupid national pride had succeeded in destroying a part of the profound impression that the rest of the spectacle had made..."

28

of the sexes. The museum has restored the apple orchard, meeting house and herb garden. The cemetery is testament to Shaker equality—all 444 tombstones are of a similar size and shape; only Mother Ann Lee's is slightly bigger. 1848 Shaker Meeting House, Albany Shaker Road. Tel: (518) 456-7890.

First Reformed Church in Albany

The name says it all. This is the oldest church in town and was originally built for the Dutch Reformed Church of Albany in 1642. This is the congregation's fourth church, designed between 1797-99 by Philip Hooker, Albany's premier architect. Tocqueville and Beaumont marched past it during their Fourth of July parade. Inside you can see Tiffany stained-glass windows and the oldest pulpit in America. Before becoming President, George Washington gave an address from the pulpit. To see the sanctuary, call for an appointment. 110 North Pearl Street. Tel: (518) 463-4449.

Tiffany window in the First Reformed Church

What to See

Shaker Heritage Society

When Tocqueville and Beaumont visited here there were close to 6,000 Shakers in the United States. Now there are just eight. The first village the Shakers settled in America is today known as Colonie. Ann Lee, the founding mother of the Shakers, came here in 1744 with a small group of followers. You can wander the grounds of the museum and learn the story of the Shaker community. Tours help shed light on some of the tenets of Shakerism including celibacy, the sharing of property and equality

Albany Institute of History and Art

The Institute is one of New York State's oldest museums. Had Tocqueville visited, he would have seen two mummies which are still on display. The Institute is an excellent place to learn about Albany history because it features everything from furniture to 18th- and 19th-century paintings of the Hudson Mohawk Valley. The Institute also features a research

Famous for their entrepreneurial skills, Shakers are credited with the invention of clothes pins and permanent press fabric.

29

Albany skyline

library and archives.
125 Washington Avenue.
Tel: (518) 463-4478.

Historic Cherry Hill

This mansion, built in 1787, was
owned by Philip Van Rensselaer,
a prosperous merchant. Four
years before Tocqueville visited
Albany, the house was the scene
of a sensational murder. Elise
Lansing Whipple, a relative of
Van Rensselaer, was living at
Cherry Hill with her husband.
She reportedly had an affair with
a hired hand who then shot her
husband. A dramatic trial
unfolded; the man was convicted
and hanged in Albany's last
public execution. His signed
confession can still be seen at
Cherry Hill. Today the mansion
showcases close to 20,000
objects including original
furnishings, books, photographs
and manuscripts.
523 1/2 South Pearl Street.
Tel: (518) 434-4791.

Ten Broeck Mansion (Arbour Hill)

The Albany County Historical
Association is housed in this
brick Federal mansion and
contains period furniture, fine
arts and Victorian bathrooms.
9 Ten Broeck Place.
Tel: (518) 436-9826.

Albany *Today*

The state capital of New York,
Albany is a commercial hub, a
growing center for the arts and
the seat of the state government.
Close to 45,000 people work
in government related jobs.
The state capitol standing today
in Empire State Plaza was
built more that thirty years
after Tocqueville left. The city
proper has a population of
more than 100,000.

Inns *and* Outs

How to get there:

Albany is about 2.5 to 3 hours
from New York City. Take the
New York State Thruway to exit
23 to Route 787 north. Follow
signs to downtown Albany.

From New England:
Take I-90 west to Route 9,
Northern Boulevard and follow
signs to Albany.

Where to stay:

Try the Albany County
Convention and Visitors Bureau
for hotel and tour information.
52 South Pearl Street,
Albany, NY 12207.
Tel: (518) 434-1217
or (800) 258-3582.

Empire State Plaza skating rink in front of the capitol

Other Attractions

The Governor Nelson A. Rockefeller Empire State Plaza

The plaza is home to Albany's famous **Egg**, the arts center designed by Wallace Harrison featuring theater, concerts, dance and film.
Tel: (518) 473-1061.

The New York State Museum exhibits focus on Native-American art, history and science. The museum offers many exhibits for children. Look for the original Big Bird and cast of other Sesame Street characters.
Tel: (518) 474-5877.

Visitors can watch the New York State legislature in session in the impressive **New York State Capitol**. It was built between 1867-99 and is now the seat of the New York State Senate and Assembly. The million-dollar staircase is carved with the faces of famous Americans. Call the **Plaza's Visitors Assistance** line for more information.
Tel: (518) 474-2418.

The Executive Mansion

The official residence of the Governor of New York, this mansion was built in 1850 and features an art collection from Revolutionary times to the present. Tours are available on Thursdays. Make reservations two weeks ahead.
138 Eagle Street.
Tel: (518) 473-7521.

The Pruyn House

This is a restored 1830s house decorated with period furnishings and exhibits. It also features a Buhrmaster barn. Located about 8-10 minutes from downtown Albany.
207 Old Niskayuna Road, Newtonville.
Tel: (518) 783-1435.

Rensselaerville

A restored 1787 village, visitors will discover 18th-century homes, inns, churches and a gristmill. 27 miles southwest via NY 443 to end of NY 85.
Tel: (518) 797-3783.

New York State Capitol in Albany

"Arrival at Utica. Charming city of 10,000 souls. Very pretty shops, founded since the war of the revolution, in the middle of an attractive plain."

—Alexis de Tocqueville

Utica
New York

In 1831, with the newly completed Erie Canal at its doorstep, Utica was a busy crossroads en route to the west. Its location, in the center of New York State along the canal route from the Atlantic to the Great Lakes, attracted thousands of new residents and expanding industries to the town. Then, as today, waterfalls, rolling hills, lakes and forests made up the area surrounding Utica. It was not far from here that James Fenimore Cooper set his classic series of novels, *The Leatherstocking Tales,* which includes *The Last of the Mohicans.*

It was from reading Cooper's tale that both Tocqueville and Beaumont came to know the bucolic country setting. In a letter to his brother, Beaumont wrote, "Here I am now, penetrating into the west. You will probably find Utica on the map...It's on the banks of the Mohawks that Cooper places *The Last of the Mohicans."*

Leatherstocking Country, the area surrounding Utica, got its name from the leather leggings worn by early settlers.

William Bartlett's sketch of Genesee and Washington Streets in 1838

32

Beaumont's memory failed him slightly. Cooper's novel was actually set around Lake George and Glens Falls, New York, about sixty miles north of Utica.

The two French nobles, traveling by stagecoach along the Mohawk trail to Auburn, stopped in Utica overnight. Tocqueville and Beaumont discovered that much had changed since Cooper penned his novels about an untamed wilderness, pioneer settlers and Indian braves only a decade before.

When Tocqueville and Beaumont arrived, Utica was a bustling city of 10,000 and the two travelers saw that the Indians of Cooper's novels were long gone. There on the evening of July 5, one day after the United States celebrated its independence and freedom, Tocqueville wrote, "One would say that the European is to the other races of men what man in general is to all animated nature. When he cannot bend them to his use or make them indirectly serve his well-being, he destroys them and makes them little by little disappear before him. The Indian races melt away in the presence of European civilization as the snow before the rays of the sun."

What to See

Erie Canal Village

Just 15 minutes from Utica in Rome, New York, is a reconstructed 1840s canal village. And near the village is the spot where work for the Erie Canal first broke ground.

Hundred-year-old buildings clustered around the canal include a tavern, a church, a blacksmith's workshop and a settler's cabin. The village also offers a boat ride down the Erie Canal, the New York State Museum of Cheese and the Erie Canal Museum. The Harden Carriage Museum exhibits antique horse-drawn vehicles. On the way to Utica, Tocqueville and Beaumont traveled for the first time in an American stagecoach. It was uncomfortable. Beaumont wrote, "the carriages are so rough that it's enough to break the toughest bones."
5789 New London Road, Rome. Tel: (315) 337-3999.

Munson-Williams-Proctor Institute

Utica's premier art institute includes a performing arts center and an extensive art collection including works by Picasso, Kandinsky and Pollock. Fountain Elms, adjacent to the institute, is an 1850s mansion designed by Philip Hooker and complete with Victorian-style furnishings. 310 Genesee Street. Tel: (315) 797-0000.

Oneida County Historical Society

The historical society operates a museum showcasing Utica and Mohawk Valley history. 1608 Genesee Street. Tel: (315) 783-1435.

Utica
Today

Utica has a population of about 20,000. Although the city has lost some industry in recent years, it is making a comeback. The Munson-Williams-Proctor Institute is a resource for the community, providing a speakers bureau and children's art programs.

To find the C-SPAN plaque marking Tocqueville's journey, visit the Ellen Hanna Park on 184 Genesee Street.

Inns and *Outs*

How to get there:

From New York City, take the New York State Thruway to exit 31-Utica. From New England, follow I-90 west to Utica.

Where to stay:

Contact the Oneida County Convention and Visitors Bureau for lodging information. PO Box 551 Utica, NY 13503. Tel: (800) 426-3132

Other Attractions

Edward A. Hanna Park

Downtown Utica's beautifully landscaped park—complete with waterfalls—is a wonderful place to relax and, during summer evenings, catch an outdoor concert.

Historic Fort Stanwix

In nearby Rome, New York, Fort Stanwix stands as a monument to Revolutionary War soldiers who withstood a British siege. The reconstructed log fort also marks the site where the Iroquois signed a treaty offering the land east of the Ohio River to the United States. Costumed guides, a film and a museum bring colonial times to life. Across the street lies the Tomb of the Unknown Soldier of the American Revolution. 112 East Park Street. Tel: (315) 336-2090.

F.X. Matt Brewing Company

Saranac beer has been brewed here for four generations. One hour after the 21st Amendment ending prohibition was signed, F.X. Matt received one of the first state licenses to brew beer. The next day he provided fresh kegs of lager to Utica. You can tour the brewery, visit the reconstructed 1888 tavern and taste free samples. Corner of Court and Varick Streets. Tel: (315) 732-0022 or (800) 765-6288.

34   Fort Stanwix, 1777

"Imagine a surface several leagues wide, water transparent and still, everywhere surrounded by thick woods whose roots it bathes, not a sail on the lake, not a house on its banks, not a wisp of smoke above the forest; perfect calm, a tranquillity as utter and complete as it should be at the beginning of the world."

—Alexis de Tocqueville on Oneida Lake

Syracuse & Fort Brewerton
New York

On their travels to Syracuse and Fort Brewerton, New York, Tocqueville and Beaumont encountered their first Indians, a prison warden and a romantic island in the middle of Oneida Lake. Beaumont, intrigued with the Indians, wrote, "...their mixed state, between savagery and a civilization not yet in existence, their relations with the Americans who push them further and further back into their forests, these will be the object of all my attention..."

In Syracuse, Tocqueville and Beaumont sought out Elam Lynds, the prison administrator who had earlier directed the building of Sing Sing prison. They interviewed Lynds about capital punishment, which he favored, and discipline, for which he advocated the whip. The two travelers also inquired about the possibility of importing Lynds' prison concepts to France. The conversation with Lynds would make its way into the prison report the Frenchmen presented to their government. They left shortly after their interview with Lynds and did not see much of Syracuse.

Instead, they were intent on following a legend about a French nobleman and his wife who had

Take a walk through Syracuse's historic Hanover Square for a look at the architecture Tocqueville may have seen in 1831. Some of the buildings date back to the 1830s and are now home to retail shops and offices.

Beaumont's sketch of Frenchman's Island

Digging In

Building the Erie Canal was backbreaking work. Workers used only picks and shovels to dig 363 miles of waterways. Canal employees were often given shots of alcohol to make it through the day.

fled France during the Reign of Terror some forty years earlier.

The nobleman had reportedly settled on an island in Oneida Lake, about 22 miles northeast of Syracuse. Tocqueville and Beaumont set off on horseback to investigate. They passed the night in Fort Brewerton on the western end of Oneida Lake in what Tocqueville called a "detestable inn." The next day, they rented a boat from a fisherman's wife who told them that she, too, had heard of the mysterious Frenchman. He had lived on the island with his wife in a little cottage, the woman explained. But his wife had died and the nobleman had simply disappeared.

> In the 1830s Syracuse, like all canal towns, was booming. The Erie Canal used to run down Erie Street but was paved over in the early 1900s.

Tocqueville and Beaumont reached the island and found it overgrown with few traces of habitation. However, beneath an apple tree, they spied the remains of a house, covered in vines. It was an adventure that Tocqueville and Beaumont never forgot. There was something about the story of a Frenchman who flees his country only to find fleeting happiness that touched them. In *Democracy in America*, Tocqueville wrote that he "stood for some time in silent admiration of the resources of Nature and the littleness of man; and when I was obliged to leave that enchanting solitude, I exclaimed with sadness, 'Are ruins, then, already here?'"

Today, Frenchman's Island, in the center of Oneida Lake, remains uninhabited. No ferries run to the island, and no bridge connects it to the mainland. A few trails, an abandoned light house and the ruins of what was once an elegant Victorian hotel are all that remain. The fishing around the island is said to be excellent.

What to See

Erie Canal Museum

The museum is housed in the Weighlock Building, the only canal boat weighing station left in the United States. Exhibits showcase the construction of the canal. The *Frank Buchanan Thomson,* a 65-foot replica, offers a glimpse of what life was like on a canal boat. The museum grounds also encompass the Old Erie Canal State Park, a 30-mile stretch of restored canal towpath and nature trails. 318 Erie Boulevard East, Syracuse. Tel: (315) 471-0593.

Sainte Marie Among the Iroquois Living History Museum

Native Americans have lived in Syracuse since the 1570s when Onondaga Chief Hiawatha chose the city as the capital of the Iroquois Confederacy. This museum is a re-creation of a 17th-century Jesuit mission, with exhibits chronicling everyday life among the Iroquois in the late 1600s. Located in Onondaga Lake Park, Rte. 370 West, Liverpool. Tel: (315) 453-6767.

36

The Salt Museum

Up until the 1870s, Syracuse, the "Salt City," provided most of the country's salt. This museum, located on the shores of Onondaga Lake, houses exhibits and artifacts from Syracuse's salt-making days including the original boiling block where salt was made. Located in Onondaga Lake Park, Rt. 370 West, Liverpool. Tel: (315) 453-6767.

Oneida Lake

The lake is 22 miles long and located a short ride from Syracuse. From Oneida Shores, a beach on the western side of the lake, you get a clear view of Frenchman's Island and can enjoy swimming during the summer. 9248 McKinley Road, Fort Brewerton.

Syracuse & Fort Brewerton *Today*

Syracuse has a population of approximately 164,000, including about 30,000 Native Americans. The Onondaga Native-American Reservation is located just south of Syracuse. The city contains Syracuse University, historic squares, scenic parks and factories that produce china, pharmaceuticals, jet engines and electronic equipment.

Inns and Outs

How to get there:

From New York City follow I-80 west towards Pennsylvania. Take 380 to I-81 north to Syracuse.

Where to stay:

For lodging information call the Syracuse Convention and Visitors Bureau. 572 South Salina Street, Syracuse, NY 13202. Tel: (315) 470-1910 or (800) 234-4797.

Other Attractions

Everson Museum of Art

The first museum designed by famed architect I.M. Pei, the Everson has an extensive collection of American paintings and ceramics. 401 Harrison Street, Syracuse. Tel: (315) 474-6064.

Onondaga Park

This charming park has been a recreational spot since the late 1890s. A fanciful footbridge and a grand old bandstand adorn the grounds. The park's Hiawatha Lake was once a favorite swimming hole. Roberts Avenue, Syracuse.

Windows on Columbus Circle Restaurant

Windows is located inside Syracuse's oldest church, the Wesleyan Methodist, built in 1846. The exterior resembles the original architecture of the church. 304 East Onondaga Street, Columbus Circle, Syracuse. Tel: (315) 424-8994.

New York State Canal Cruises & Mid-Lakes Navigation Co.

Cruises along the Onondaga portion of the Canal are available. Tel: (315) 685-8500 or (800) 545-4318.

Look for the C-SPAN plaque in the northwestern corner of Syracuse's Hanover Square.

"At Auburn here, we are in a magnificent hotel placed in the middle of a small town of 2,000 souls, all of whose houses have well furnished shops. Auburn is to-day the centre of an immense commerce. Twenty years ago they hunted deer and bear here at their ease."

—Alexis de Tocqueville

Auburn
New York

Auburn is famous for its prison, a freedom runner and a statesman. After escaping from slavery and guiding others to freedom, as well as serving as a spy in the Civil War, Harriet Tubman made her home here. William Seward, Lincoln's Secretary of State who headed negotiations with Russia to purchase "Seward's Folly," better known as Alaska, settled here too. Today you can tour both of their houses. But it was for the "Big House"—the State Penitentiary—that Tocqueville and Beaumont came to Auburn in 1831.

Intent on gathering research for their prison report, the two French commissioners spent five days studying the Auburn State Penitentiary. When they arrived, Auburn was in the midst of a growth spurt. The penitentiary, which had opened in 1816, provided cheap prison labor for construction and road building, thus paving the way for industry to enter the town.

But vast farmland and the Finger Lakes still surrounded Auburn. Tocqueville and Beaumont took in some of the scenery during their visit to Governor Enos T. Throop's country house. The Frenchmen had met the Governor twice before, first in New York City and later when they marched

38 Early sketch of Auburn State Prison, founded in 1816

Attempted Murder

William Seward barely escaped assassination in the same plot that succeeded against President Lincoln. On April 14th, 1865, Seward was in bed, in his Washington, DC home, recovering from a carriage accident. Lewis Payne, a confederate of John Wilkes Booth, made his way into Seward's bedroom under the pretense of bringing a prescription. Payne stabbed Seward in the face and neck with a knife. He ran out of the house but was caught and later hanged. The neckbrace Seward wore as a result of the carriage accident helped save his life.

with him in Albany's Fourth of July parade. Beaumont described their visit in a letter to his sister. "He [Governor Throop] has little money; the state gives him only twenty thousand francs as salary, which is very little for a man in his position...He took us for a walk in his woods. While admiring the beauty of the trees we caught sight of a squirrel. At that the governor began to run as fast as his legs would carry him to get his gun at the house. He soon came back, all out of breath, with his murderous weapon. The small animal had had the patience to wait for him, but the big man had the clumsiness to miss him four times in succession."

Tocqueville and Beaumont were not impressed. How could it be that the top-ranking official of the state of New York made such a miserable salary that he also had to cultivate a farm to make a living? The Frenchmen discussed this with Elam Lynds, the founder of the Auburn Penitentiary. Lynds told Tocqueville he believed that low salaries kept men with "distinction" from running for office. Upon his return to France, Tocqueville wrote in *Democracy in America,* "In our day it is a constant fact that the most outstanding Americans are

seldom summoned to public office, and it must be recognized that this tendency has increased as democracy has gone beyond its previous limits. It is clear that during the last fifty years the race of American statesmen has strangely shrunk."

What to See

Cayuga Museum of History and Art & Case Research Lab

Housed in the Greek-Revival Willard and Case Mansion, the museum is furnished with 19th-century antiques and has exhibits on local history including a collection on Native-American culture, a Tiffany window and displays on women's histories in Cayuga County. The **Case Research Lab,** located in the converted greenhouse on the museum grounds, is the lab where motion picture sound was invented. The first sound camera and projector, lab equipment and early test films are on display. 203 Genesee Street. Tel: (315) 253-8051.

The prison that Tocqueville and Beaumont visited in 1831 still operates, but it is now called the Auburn Correctional Facility. Through the years, the penitentiary has survived policy changes and riots. Today it is a maximum security jail housing 1,600 inmates and is not open to the public.

The Seward House today

Seward House

William Seward, former Governor of New York in 1838 and Abraham Lincoln's Secretary of State, lived in this mansion with his family for seventy years. A 15-year-old Brigham Young, then a painter and a carpenter who later became a founding leader of the Mormon Church, helped build the house. The 30-room mansion is filled with antique furnishings and articles from Seward's life including his uniform as Governor, a certificate of appointment as Secretary of State signed by Abraham Lincoln and Alaskan artifacts. 33 South Street. Tel: (315) 252-1283.

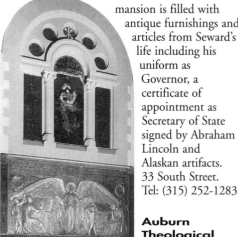

Stained-glass window in Willard Memorial Chapel

Auburn Theological Seminary

Tocqueville and Beaumont visited the old seminary and talked to Rev. James Richards, a professor, about the importance of morals in a democracy. The Willard Memorial Chapel and the attached Welch Memorial Building are all that remain of the seminary. In 1939 the seminary moved to New York City. The beautiful interior of the Willard Memorial Chapel was designed by Tiffany Glass and Decorating Company and is said to be the only untouched Tiffany Chapel still in existence. Open Tuesday through Friday, April through December and by appointment. 17 Nelson Street. Tel: (315) 252-0339.

Harriet Tubman House

Born a slave in the 1820s, Harriet Tubman escaped to Canada only to make her way back down South to lead nearly 300 slaves to freedom. After the Civil War, in which Tubman served as a spy, a nurse and a scout, she settled in this house. The tour includes Tubman's house and a home for aged and indigent blacks that Tubman operated after the war. 180 South Street. Tel: (315) 252-2081.

Inns *and* Outs

How to get there:

From the south, take I-80 west toward Pennsylvania, follow to I-380. Stay on I-380 to I-8I north. From there, pick up US 20 (the Cherry Valley Turnpike) and continue on to Auburn.

From the north, take I-90 west to I-481 south. Pick up I-690 west and follow to State Rt. 695 south. Pick up State Rt. 5 and continue on until you reach Auburn.

40

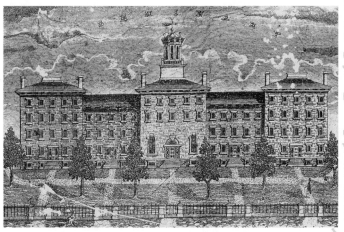
Sketch of Auburn Theological Seminary, founded in 1819

Where to stay:
For hotel information contact the Cayuga County Office of Tourism.
151 Genesee Street, Auburn, NY 13021.
Tel: (800) 499-9615.

Other Attractions

Fort Hill Cemetery
Set on a high hill overlooking Auburn, this cemetery, once a Native-American burial ground, is the final resting place for Auburn's most famous citizens. Look for the 56-foot-high monument honoring Logan, a famous Iroquois chief. The monument was erected on an ancient earthwork structure built by Cayuga Iroquois Indians. Harriet Tubman and William Seward are also buried here. 9 Fort Street.

Owasco Teyetasta (Iroquois) Native American Museum/Emerson Park
Designed as a "long house," this museum's collections reflect the culture of the Iroquois and traditional Northeast Woodlands native people. You can also see a 12,000-year-old mastodon skeleton. The museum is open only during summer months. Rt. 38A. Tel: (315) 253-8051. Across the street from the museum is Emerson Park with rolling lawns overlooking Owasco Lake, where summer visitors can enjoy beaches, boating and children's rides.

Cayuga County Agricultural Museum
The agricultural museum is devoted to bringing homestead living in the early 1900s to life and features antique tractors, a farm kitchen, a workshop, a creamery, a veterinarian's office, a general store and an herb garden. Located opposite the entrance to Emerson Park on Rt. 38A. Open Memorial through Labor Day. Tel: (315) 252-7644.

Look for the C-SPAN plaque on William and South Streets, adjacent to the William Seward House.

"My third Lake is Lake Cananda[i]gua which has given its name to a small town near by where I am at this moment. This last lake is the prettiest of the three; perhaps even above all those I have seen to date."

—Gustave de Beaumont

Canandaigua
New York

Situated on a beautiful Finger Lake bordered by vineyards, Canandaigua is an agreeable place to visit, especially in warm weather. Tourists can enjoy steamboat rides, swimming, boating and fishing on the lake. Tocqueville and Beaumont came to Canandaigua on July 16, in time to relish some of upstate New York's fine summer weather.

In 1831, Canandaigua was a small town with wide, tree-lined streets and Federal-style houses. Just a few years before the two French travelers arrived, the town had been a gateway to the west and the frontier. It was a transportation center before the construction of the Erie Canal.

Today the Spencer house still stands on 210 North Main and is now the Elm Manor Nursing Home.

The two travelers spent a few days with John Canfield Spencer and his family in their home. Spencer was a district attorney, congressman and later became Secretary of War under President John Tyler. Tocqueville and Beaumont were intrigued with Spencer's thoughts and his two pretty daughters. Tocqueville described his host as a "very distinguished jurist...The nature of his mind seems to be clearness and perspicacity."

Spencer and his guests talked of many things, including the American press, the separation of the House and Senate, and public education. It is evident that much of what Spencer talked about with Tocqueville found its way into *Democracy in America*.

Spencer told Tocqueville that one way to check the power of the press was to "multiply the number of newspapers as far as possible." Tocqueville later wrote, "it is an axiom of political science there that the only way to neutralize the effect of newspapers is to multiply their numbers."

John Canfield Spencer's home

42

The Beginnings of Billy Budd

At the age of 18, Philip Spencer, son of John Spencer, was convicted of mutiny and hung at sea in a sensational incident that rocked the nation. After short terms at Hobart, Geneva, and Union Colleges, Philip enlisted in the Navy. He was ordered aboard the *U.S. Somers*, a training ship headed for Africa. The Commander ran a tight ship, and differing accounts said Spencer either was merely defying authority or actually planning to murder the officers. The Commander put Spencer in shackles, and officers aboard ship found him and two other crew members guilty. Spencer and his comrades were hanged December 1, 1842. Public outcry resulted, and Herman Melville, who was related to the Commander of the *U.S. Somers*, would later base his classic story *Billy Budd* on the incident.

In the end, it was Spencer's two beautiful daughters and the temptation they provided that drove the Frenchmen away.

Tocqueville tells his sister-in-law in a letter, "you have scarce seen their like on the other side of the water. I would describe them to you, were I not afraid of being insipid. Let it suffice you to know that we gazed on them even more willingly than on the books of the father. Having confided this discovery to each other, Beau. and I resolved, with all the sagacity which characterizes us, to be on our way as soon as possible..."

The *Canandaigua Lady*

Captain Gray's Boat Tours

Another chance to explore the Canandaigua shoreline by water, Captain Gray's offers narrated tours chronicling the lives of the Seneca Native Americans who first settled the area. 770 South Main Street. Tel: (716) 394-5270.

Sonnenberg Gardens & Mansion

This 40-room mansion was the former summer home of Mary and Frederick Thompson. The house and its extensive gardens, including Japanese, Moonlight

What to See

The *Canandaigua Lady* Cruises

On this replica of a 19th-century steamboat, a narrated tour tells you about both the Native-American and vineyard history of Canandaigua. You also have a chance to pilot the boat. Spring cruises board at North End Docksite, 169 Lakeshore Drive, Canandaigua. Fall cruises board at South End Docksite, Route 21 South, Woodville. Tel: (716) 394-5365.

Canandaigua Lake

Sonnenberg Gardens

and Butterfly gardens, are open for tours. The mansion is located at 151 Charlotte Street. Tel: (716) 394-4922.

Granger Homestead & Carriage Museum

Built in 1816, this Federal-style house was owned by Gideon Granger who was Postmaster General under Thomas Jefferson. The Carriage Museum contains forty-four horse-drawn vehicles, including carriages, sleighs, coaches, commercial wagons and even an undertaker's hearse. 295 North Main Street. Tel: (716) 394-1472.

Ontario County Historical Society

The society features changing exhibits on local history and has a children's discovery room with books, activities and games as well as a historical archive. 55 North Main Street. Tel: (716) 394-4975.

Canandaigua *Today*

This town with its population of more than 10,000, still retains some of the elegance of old. The Public Square contains some fine examples of Federal-style architecture including City Hall. Wineries and water sports help to make tourism Canandaigua's primary growth industry.

Inns *and* Outs

How to get there:
From Buffalo, New York, take New York State Thruway east to Canandaigua, exit 44. Take Route 332 south to Canandaigua.

Where to stay:
Try the Canandaigua Chamber of Commerce for hotel information. 113 South Main Street. Canandaigna, NY 14424. Tel: (716) 394-4400. Also try the Ontario County Tourism Promotions Agency. 248 South Main Street, Canandaigna, NY 14424. Tel: (716) 394-3915.

44 Ontario County Courthouse

"...Buffalo. Pretty shops. French goods. Refinement of European luxury."
—Alexis de Tocqueville

Buffalo
New York

Situated at the tip of Lake Erie and the Niagara River, Buffalo's greatest natural resource has always been its waterways. When Tocqueville and Beaumont arrived in Buffalo, the Erie Canal had just opened and steamboats were continuously crossing the lake. Today you can tour the Buffalo waterways on an excursion boat or travel through the original locks which helped propel the city into a transportation and manufacturing hub.

On their first walk around town, the two men encountered a group of intoxicated Native Americans who had just received annuity payments for lands they had ceded to the U.S. Tocqueville was bitterly disappointed with the sight. "I was expecting to find the natives of America savages, but savages on whose face nature had stamped the marks of some of the proud virtues which liberty brings forth. I expected to find a race of men little different from Europeans, whose bodies had been developed by the strenuous exercise of hunting and of war," he wrote.

Instead he saw Indians dressed in an odd mix of European and traditional clothing, with men in some cases wearing women's garments. In the road, he saw an Indian woman rolling in the dust "uttering savage cries" and

> Tocqueville and Beaumont stayed in a hotel, probably at the foot of Main Street, near the current location of the Marine Midland Arena.

Buffalo waterfront, 1825

45

Buffalo, New York

No Buffalo in Buffalo

The origin of the city's name remains a mystery. There have never been any wild buffalo, that is American bison, in Buffalo. Instead historians suspect that the name may come from a mispronunciation of the French *beau fleuve* or "beautiful river."

another young man passed out.

Throughout their travels through the American frontier and into the deep South, Tocqueville and Beaumont would continue to observe, investigate and, in the end, become deeply troubled about the treatment of American Indians. In *Democracy in America*, Tocqueville wrote that oppression had been fatal to the Native American. "Before the arrival of white men in the New World, the inhabitants of North America lived quietly in their woods ... The Europeans, having dispersed the Indian tribes and driven them into the deserts, condemned them to a wandering life, full of inexpressible sufferings."

What to See

Miss Buffalo/Niagara Clipper Cruises

The *Miss Buffalo* tour boat shows you the magnificent Buffalo waterfront and passes through historic Black Rock Lock and Canal. Sights include the Buffalo Lighthouse, built in 1833, Old Fort Erie and the Peace Bridge which spans across the Niagara River from Buffalo to Canada. 79 Marine Drive. Tel: (716) 856-6696.

Wilcox Mansion

In this Greek-Revival mansion, Theodore Roosevelt was sworn in as the nation's 26th President following the assassination of

The Holland Land Office, early 1800s

William McKinley on September 14, 1901. Tours of the furnished mansion tell the story of the inauguration (which took place in the library) and give visitors a look back to Victorian times. 641 Delaware Avenue. Tel: (716) 884-0095.

Buffalo Naval and Military Park

At Buffalo's Naval and Military Park you can take a tour of a guided missile cruiser, a destroyer and a World War II submarine. Museum pieces also include uniforms and other memorabilia. One Naval Park Cove. Tel: (716) 847-1773.

Buffalo and Erie County Historical Society

The historical society is housed in a Greek-Revival building that was designed as the New York State Building during the Pan-American Exposition of 1901. It was at the exposition that President William McKinley was fatally shot. The museum features exhibits on Buffalo's early settlers as well as German, Irish and Italian immigrants who later made the city their home. More than 700 artifacts,

including Fisher-Price toys and an electronic pacemaker, chronicle Buffalo's manufacturing history. 25 Nottingham Court. Tel: (716) 873-9644.

Holland Land Company

Tocqueville journeyed through Batavia on his way to Buffalo. He likely passed the prominent Holland Land Office which was the headquarters for six Dutch banking firms that sold off 3.5 million acres of western New York land. Built in 1815, the museum houses artifacts which chronicle the history of Batavia and Genesee County. 131 West Main Street, Batavia. Tel: (716) 343-4727.

> On his way to Buffalo, Tocqueville wrote that the population around Batavia was sparse. The land at the time was primarily marshy wetlands and the road rutted and pitted with tree trunks.

Buffalo
Today

Buffalo, the second largest city in the state, is known for football, its blizzards and spicy chicken wings. The city offers examples of magnificent architectural design, including five houses designed by Frank Lloyd Wright and elegant city parks designed by Frederick Law Olmsted, the mastermind of New York City's Central Park. Home to eighteen colleges including the University of Buffalo, more than 300,000 people live in Buffalo.

Exit 7 (Church Street) leads to downtown Buffalo.

Where to stay:
For lodging information contact the Greater Buffalo Convention & Visitors Bureau. 617 Main Street, Buffalo, NY 14203. Tel: (716) 852-0511 or (888) 2BUFFNY.

Inns *and* Outs

How to get there:
Take the New York State Thruway (I-90) to exit 53 (I90 north).

Other Attractions

Albright-Knox Art Gallery
More than 6,000 works are housed in the gallery. The collection has an emphasis on the 20th century. Pieces by Picasso, Braque, Matisse and Mondrian are on permanent display. 1285 Elmwood Avenue. Tel: (716) 882-8700.

Lockport Locks and Erie Canal Cruises
Take a two-hour narrated cruise through the only set of double locks in the Erie Canal. Widewaters Marina, Market Street, Lockport.
Tel: (716) 693-3260 or (800) 378-0352.

Buffalo Zoological Gardens
Situated on 23 acres in Delaware Park, the Buffalo Zoo dates back to 1875 and has over 1,000 animals including an albino alligator and a rare white tiger. 300 Parkside Avenue. Tel: (716) 837-3900.

48   City Hall

> *"At 9 o'clock in the morning we touched at Erie, founded by the French under the name of 'Presqu'île.' Now the lake has opened a passage between the mainland and the peninsula and made the latter into an island."*
>
> —Alexis de Tocqueville

Erie
Pennsylvania

Erie's Presque Isle peninsula, which juts into the cool waters of Lake Erie, offers great swimming, hiking and lots of history along its seven miles of sandy beaches. According to Indian legend, the Eriez Nation was led here by the Great Spirit with the promise that the area would be a land of plenty. The peninsula's name, Presque Isle, came from the French meaning "almost" or "close to" an island. Several times over the last century, storm waves crashed over the narrow neck of the peninsula and isolated it from the mainland. When Tocqueville came to Erie on July 21, 1831, the area was an island.

Tocqueville and Beaumont were on a steamboat heading for Detroit and points west when they stopped in Erie. They arrived in the midst of a downpour and the Frenchmen stayed for only an hour. But Tocqueville still managed to note the construction of a canal, about which he wrote, "the riches of Europe will circulate freely across the five hundred leagues of land which separate the Gulf of Mexico from the Atlantic Ocean."

Since the famed Erie Canal was completed in 1825, what Tocqueville probably saw was the construction of the Erie and Pittsburgh Canal which was completed in 1844. Tocqueville was clearly impressed with America's commerce. In *Democracy in America*, he penned, "I cannot express my thoughts better than by saying that the Americans put something heroic into their way of trading."

During the War of 1812, which pitted the United States against Great Britain, Misery Bay, on the peninsula's southeast side, was home port to Commodore Oliver Hazard Perry's fleet. During the war, many of Perry's men died from smallpox and were buried in nearby Grave Yard Pond.

U.S. Brig Niagara

Perry Luck

Luck was with Commodore Oliver Hazard Perry the fateful day of September 10, 1813, during the Battle of Lake Erie. His mission was to wrest control of Lake Erie from the British. Perry and his brother were the only two officers to escape unharmed from his sinking flagship, *Lawrence*. Perry's dog, which he had hidden in a cabinet, survived a cannon blast. After transferring to the ship *Niagara*, Perry and his crew single-handedly defeated the British fleet. It was the first time in history that an entire British squadron was captured. Perry later reported his victory with the famous line, "We have met the enemy and they are ours..." His men dubbed his good fortune "Perry Luck."

What to See

U.S. Brig Niagara

This man-o-war is a reconstruction of Perry's victorious ship built to commemorate the Battle of Lake Erie's 175th anniversary. The official flagship of Pennsylvania, it tours Lake Erie and the Pennsylvania shoreline. When in port, the *Niagara* is open for tours. Located at the foot of Holland Street. Tel: (814) 871-4596.

50 Oliver Hazard Perry

Dickson Tavern

Erie's oldest surviving building, the tavern dates back to the early 1800s. The Marquis de Lafayette was honored here with a banquet in 1825. John Dickson, a veteran sailor, owned this tavern when Erie's main shipping pier was at the foot of French Street. Before the Civil War, the tavern was a stop on the underground railroad. Today, the tavern is a historic museum honoring Erie's hero, Oliver Hazard Perry. Open weekends during the summer months. 201 French Street. Tours can be arranged by Erie's City Parks Department. Tel: (814) 870-1452.

Presque Isle State Park

The park is so large (3,200 acres in all) that it easily accommodates the more than four million people who visit it each year. There are beaches, hiking trails and a lighthouse built in 1872. At Crystal Point, look for the monument erected to Perry. The park is located off of PA Route 832. Tel: (814) 833-7424. Across the main street is Waldameer Park and Water World with a 100-foot gondola ferris wheel. 220 Peninsula Drive. Tel: (814) 838-3591.

Lighthouse in Presque Isle State Park

Erie
Today

Erie is a busy port city of more than 100,000 residents. Lumber, coal, petroleum, grain, chemicals and iron are all shipped out of Erie's waterfront. Local industry includes the manufacturing of electrical equipment, aluminum, clothing, chemicals and rubber products.

Inns and Outs

How to get there:
From the north take I-90 west toward Pennsylvania, follow to State Route 430 northwest. Pick up US 20 southwest to Erie. From the south, take the Pennsylvania Turnpike (I-76) to I-79 (exit 3). Follow I-79 north to Erie.

Where to stay:
For lodging information contact the Erie Area Chamber of

Commerce/Convention and Visitors Bureau. 1006 State Street, Erie, PA 16501. Tel: (814) 454-7191.

Other Attractions

Erie Historical Museum and Planetarium
Housed in the grand Watson-Curtze mansion, with its stained-glass windows and ornate flourishes, this museum focuses on regional and maritime history. A children's playroom contains a trunk full of old-style clothes that children can play dress up with, an 1872 doll house and computer games about Victorian times. The planetarium is located in the old carriage house. 356 West 6th Street. Tel: (814) 871-5790 (museum); (814) 871-5794 (planetarium).

Erie Art Museum
Located in the Old Customs House, the Erie Art Museum contains a fine collection which includes American ceramics, Japanese prints and Indian bronzes. 411 State Street. Tel: (814) 459-5477.

Look for the C-SPAN plaque on Bicentennial Tower at the foot of State Street.

Fishing at Presque Isle State Park

51

> *"One goes without transition from the wilds into a city street, from the most savage scenes to the most smiling pictures of civilised life. If you are not caught by nightfall and forced to lodge at the foot of a tree, you are sure to come to a place where you will find everything, even French fashions and Palais Royal caricatures."*
>
> —Alexis de Tocqueville

Cleveland
Ohio

Unspoiled stretches of virgin forest, the noble Indians of James Fenimore Cooper's novels—those were the sights Tocqueville and Beaumont longed to see.

Perhaps they had come to America too late. The frontier the two were looking for had continued to slip westward. People told them of cutting down the first trees and conferring with the leaders of the great Iroquois nation, but Tocqueville and Beaumont wanted to experience the American frontier for themselves. Tocqueville, in his quest to understand the American character, suspected the frontier had something to do with American prosperity. Thus when they discovered that steamships regularly ran from Buffalo to Detroit—a gateway to the frontier—the Frenchmen booked passage on the *Ohio*. On July 19, 1831, they set off across Lake Erie, bound for the wilderness.

En route to Detroit, the *Ohio* stopped in Cleveland for just an hour. There, on the fringes of civilization, stood a

Bank and St. Clair Streets in Cleveland, 1833

town that could have been transplanted straight from the East Coast. There were steepled churches and elegant homes such as the Nicholson House in Lakewood that still stands today. Canals completed during the 1830s brought trade, products and people to the city and the population skyrocketed. The 1830 census showed 1,075 people in Cleveland. By 1840, the count had reached 6,071. The canals made the town an important shipping center. Later, the railroad would end the canal era, but Cleveland, situated between New York City and Chicago, would remain prosperous.

Today, Cleveland is home to more than 20 major industrial corporations. In recent years, the city has poured a lot of time, money and effort into developing its cultural resources.

Tocqueville was in Cleveland for a short time, but he may have guessed that the town would continue to grow. America was expanding westward, and as Tocqueville wrote in *Democracy in America,* there would be a continual stream of "...pioneers, who pierce the woods, scare off the beasts of prey, explore the courses of the inland streams, and make ready the triumphal march of civilization..."

What to See

Steamship William G. Mather Museum

Although built a century after Tocqueville visited, this floating museum gives a detailed account of shipping on the Great Lakes. 1001 East Ninth Street Pier. Tel: (216) 574-6262.

Dunham Tavern Museum

Tocqueville and Beaumont came to Cleveland by water, but others of the period traveled over land. Built in 1824, Dunham Tavern became the hub of Old Cleveland. Today the museum is a restoration of a stagecoach stop between Detroit and Buffalo. Open Wednesdays and Sundays. 6709 Euclid Avenue. Tel: (216) 431-1060.

Hale Farm and Village

Costumed pioneers tell the story of 1830s life on the frontier. Twenty-one buildings, including a blacksmith shop, a bakery, a sawmill, orchards and a garden make up the village. Craftspeople blow glass and make pottery, brooms and candles. 2686 Oak Hill Road, Bath. Tel: (330) 666-3711.

Western Reserve Historical Society

Located in University Circle—Cleveland's museum and cultural cluster—the Historical Society is housed in two turn-of-the-century mansions. The Hay-McKinney House was built by President Garfield's son and contains a collection of artifacts from the well-to-do family that lived here. The *Crossroads* exhibit traces the history of Cleveland from its founding by Moses Cleaveland to the introduction of the canals and railroads. The library has a wide collection of manuscripts focusing on Ohio labor and its impact on American history. The Frederick

The city was named for its founder Moses Cleaveland, who laid the ground work for the town in 1796. The city's name was spelled with an "a" until the newspaper *The Cleveland Gazette and Commercial Register* had to drop a letter to get its name to fit on the masthead. An editor at the *Gazette* chose the "a" and thus Cleaveland became Cleveland.

Downtown Cleveland

C. Crawford Auto Aviation Museum features everything from Model T's to modern cars. 10825 East Boulevard. Tel: (216) 721-5722.

Oldest Stone House Museum

Just a few minutes drive from Cleveland, this house gives visitors a feel for Cleveland's pioneer past. Erected in 1838 by John Honam, it is an example of one of the first homes built to replace the log cabins of the earlier settlers. Look for the horsehair sofa, roped beds and the sick or "borning" room. Lakewood is immediately west of Cleveland, off of US Highway Alt. 6, along Lake Erie. The museum is operated by the Lakewood Historical Society. 14710 Lake Avenue, Lakewood. Tel: (216) 221-7343.

Nicholson House

Also run by the Lakewood Historical Society, the Nicholson House is a fine example of the New England-style architecture that moved west. The house was built in 1835 by James Nicholson who also helped construct the first school house in the area. 13335 Detroit Avenue, Lakewood. Tel: (216) 221-7343.

Cleveland *Today*

Today 500,000 people live in Cleveland proper. Tourist attractions such as the Rock and Roll Hall of Fame and Jacobs Field draw millions of music and sports fans annually. The Lake Erie and the Cuyahoga River waterfronts have been cleaned up and are flourishing, offering a number of tourist attractions, cafés, stores and museums. The Flats, a newly developed area, is one of Cleveland's thriving entertainment spots.

Inns and Outs

How to get there:

I-90 brings you into the heart of Cleveland. Routes from the south include SR 8, SR 21 and US 42.

Where to stay:

For lodging suggestions, contact the Convention and Visitors Bureau of Greater Cleveland. 50 Public Square, Terminal Tower, Suite 3100, Cleveland, OH 44113. Tel: (800) 321-1004. Or, call the Visitors Hotline. Tel: (216) 621-4110.

54

Other Attractions

The Flats

Once a heavy industrial district, The Flats is now the entertainment mecca for downtown Cleveland. You can find the newest nightclubs, restaurants and stores along the Cuyahoga River. For more information call the Visitors Bureau.
Tel: (216) 621-5555.

Rock and Roll Hall of Fame

John Lennon's multi-colored Rolls-Royce, Jimi Hendrix's handwritten lyrics and stage costumes from Iggy Pop are all housed in the Hall of Fame. The museum has films, exhibits and interactive displays documenting the world of rock and roll.
1 Key Plaza. Tel: (216) 781-7625.

The Cleveland Museum of Art

The museum is well known for its medieval European collection, Egyptian art and paintings. Located in University Circle on 11150 East Boulevard. Tel: (216) 421-7340.

The Cleveland Playhouse Square Center

Cleveland's original theater district, built in 1921-22, is home to the Cleveland Ballet, Opera and Great Lakes Theater Festival. 1501 Euclid Avenue. Tel: (216) 771-4444 for general information; (216) 241-6000 for ticketing.

The Great Lakes Science Center

Next door to the Rock and Roll Hall of Fame is a museum where you can touch a tornado and climb onto a bridge of fire where 2,000 volts of electricity cause your hair to stand on end. The Great Lakes Science Center is devoted to science, technology and the environment with a special emphasis on how all three affect the Great Lakes. 601 Erieside Avenue. Tel: (216) 694-2000.

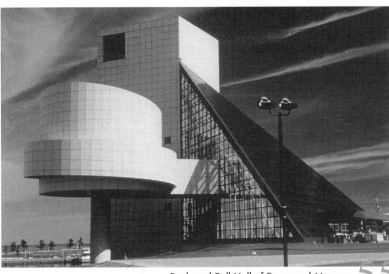

Rock and Roll Hall of Fame and Museum

"Under the trees on the bank, huts of a sort with a fire in the middle. Naked children around. On one side extreme civilisation, on the other the extreme opposite."

—Alexis de Tocqueville

Detroit
Michigan

Tocqueville and Beaumont were greeted by contrasting sights when they entered Detroit on July 22, 1831. From the deck of their steamship, they saw a soldier, standing on the river bank, fully dressed in traditional Scottish garb, complete with a feather in his hat. On the opposite bank, two Indians "entirely naked, their bodies streaked with paint, their noses pierced by rings," cast off in a wooden canoe with a blanket for a sail. The small boat, carried by the current, headed toward the Scottish soldier, "who, still shining and motionless, seemed placed there as the representative of the brilliant and armed civilization of Europe."

In 1701, Antoine de la Mothe Cadillac landed in Detroit—where the downtown Civic Center now stands—and built a fur trading post. From then on, the city used its natural resources to grow into one of the foremost industrial centers of the nation.

For the Frenchmen, this brief tableau illustrated the contrast of two civilizations. In Detroit, on the fringes of the frontier, cultures mixed regularly.

When Tocqueville and Beaumont arrived, there was still a French influence in the town. The area was originally settled by the French in an attempt to hold back British expansion. Detroit remained under the French until 1760 when the British finally won the city as a result of the French and Indian War.

Tocqueville and Beaumont passed through Detroit primarily because it was a way station en route to the wilderness. But before heading west, they made one stop. As far away as New York, Tocqueville and Beaumont had heard of Gabriel Richard, a Catholic priest. Father Richard had escaped from France during

Detroit from Sandwich Point, 1837

56

Detroit, Michiagn

Detroit Firsts

Detroit, the city of cars, has been making automotive history since 1896, when Henry Ford built his first car here. The Motor City also installed the first traffic light (1915), paved the first concrete road (1909) and built the first urban freeway in the nation (1942).

the French Revolution and made his way to Detroit. He devoted all his energy to the city, founding *The Observer*, Michigan's first paper, co-founding the University of Michigan and serving as a member of Congress.

Tocqueville and Beaumont stopped at St. Anne's church, now located on 1000 Saint Anne Street, to talk with the old priest about religious tolerance. They were grateful for Richard's insights as he helped shed light on the role of religion in America.

After the interview, the two travelers set out to explore the wilderness. It proved more difficult than they expected. Detroiters could not understand why the two wanted to see the frontier. They "will gladly send you off to see a road, a bridge, or a fine village. But that one should appreciate great trees and the beauties of solitude—that possibility completely passes him by," wrote Tocqueville.

So the Frenchmen resorted to trickery. Under the guise of looking to buy land, they approached Major John Biddle, the registrar for Detroit's land office. Biddle suggested they look at some of the more settled areas. Tocqueville thanked him for the information and then off-handedly asked him the places to avoid. Biddle warned him to steer away from the undeveloped area of Saginaw, where only "wild beasts and Indians are to be found."

The next day, Tocqueville and Beaumont rented two horses and, with guns swung over their shoulders and straw hats on their heads, set out for Saginaw and the wilds of the American frontier.

What to See

Detroit Historical Museum

This museum takes a look at Detroit's history from all angles. The *Furs to Factories* exhibit traces Detroit's growth from a sleepy outpost to a world industrial capital. Step into the *Streets of Detroit,* a re-creation of Detroit's store fronts from 1840 to 1900, for a glimpse of what Detroit looked like when Tocqueville visited.

The *Motor City Exhibition* allows you to "design" a car or choose a job on the assembly line and provides an overview of the city's automotive history. On the second floor, *Doorway to Freedom* chronicles Detroit's part in the Underground Railroad. Detroit was one of the last stops in America before escaped slaves reached Canada.

The museum also contains a toy gallery and a fashion library. 5401 Woodward Avenue, across from the Detroit Institute of the Arts. Tel: (313) 833-1805.

For more on the city's industrial growth, visit the Detroit Historical Museum's exhibit *Furs to Factories: Detroit at Work, 1701 to 1901.*

Cityscape of Detroit

St. Anne's Catholic Church

Tocqueville stopped at St. Anne's when he visited Father Gabriel Richard. Established in 1701, when Antoine de la Mothe Cadillac founded Detroit, it was one of the first log structures built. St. Anne's has been housed in eight different buildings.

When Tocqueville and Beaumont came to town, St. Anne's stood on the corner of Larned and Bates Street. Today St. Anne's is housed in a Gothic-style church (built in 1886), two blocks east of the Ambassador Bridge.

Father Gabriel Richard's body is interred in the church. He died when the plague swept through Detroit in the summer of 1832, a year after meeting Tocqueville and Beaumont. Richard formed a nursing corps but was struck ill and became one of the last victims of the plague.

The church contains some of the oldest church records in the United States. As you enter, look up at the gargoyles that guard the front door.
1000 Saint Anne Street.
Tel: (313) 496-1701.

Detroit
Today

Detroit remains an industrial city with a long, rich history. Almost one million people live in the city proper, and nearly four million people live in the metropolitan area.

Today, Detroit boasts a culturally diverse population, with more than 150 ethnic groups living in the metropolitan area. The city reaps the benefits with a myriad of good ethnic restaurants. Visit Greektown, on Monroe Avenue, for authentic Greek food. Dearborn, just a few minutes away from downtown, offers a variety of Middle Eastern restaurants.

Motown Records, renowned for the 1960s sounds of the Supremes, the Four Tops and Marvin Gaye, was founded in Detroit, but it is the car that put the city on the world map. In 1903, Henry Ford started the Ford Motor Company and made his dream of mass producing cars a reality.

58

Inns *and* Outs

How to get there:
1-75 takes you into Detroit from the north and south. From the west and northeast take I-94.

Where to stay:
The Metropolitan Detroit Convention and Visitors Bureau can point you toward hotels and provide additional information. 100 Renaissance Center, Suite 1900, Detroit, MI 48243. Tel: (800) Detroit (800-338-7648). www.visitdetroit.com.

Other Attractions

Henry Ford Museum and Greenfield Village
In this large indoor/outdoor museum you can find everything from the rocking chair Abraham Lincoln sat in the night he was shot at Ford's Theater to Charles Lindburgh's motorcycle. You'll also see a letter that Clyde Barrow, of Bonnie and Clyde infamy, wrote to Ford, praising him on his "dandy" automobile. The museum details America's growth from a rural to an industrial society.

During your visit, stop by the Eagle Tavern. The tavern was built the year Tocqueville visited and was originally located on the Detroit-Chicago road in Clinton, Michigan. Henry Ford purchased the building in 1927 and moved it to Greenfield Village. Today the tavern serves authentic 19th-century food including pork, mutton and beef. You can also sample a modern version of a mid-1800s cocktail. The museum and the village are next to each other.

20900 Oakwood Boulevard, Dearborn. Tel: (313) 271-1620.

Belle Isle
Belle Isle, located on the island in the middle of Detroit River, is a 1,000-acre park featuring the nation's oldest aquarium, a zoo and a conservatory. The Dossin Great Lakes Museum chronicles maritime development on the Great Lakes. Look for models of 1830s steamships to get a feel for the steamers that carried Tocqueville and Beaumont across the Great Lakes. The MacArthur Bridge leads to the island. Tel: (313) 852-4076.

Motown Historical Museum
Hitsville USA is located in the old two-story house of Motown founder Berry Gordy. The museum traces Motown's founding and rise to success. Visit Studio A where such classic hits as "Dancin' in the Streets" and "My Girl" were recorded. 2648 West Grand Boulevard. Tel: (313) 875-2264.

Eastern Market
Built in 1891, Detroit's historic market makes for good food shopping. Located downtown on Gratiot Avenue and Russell Street.

Old Mariner's Church
170 East Jefferson Avenue. Tel: (313) 259-2206.

Museum of African-American History
315 East Warren Avenue. Tel: (313) 494-5800

Lake Clair

> *"Twenty very clean and very pretty houses, making up as many well-furnished shops; a transparent stream; a clearing of a quarter of a league square; and the everlasting forest all around; that is a true picture of the village of Pontiac which in twenty years perhaps—will be a town."*
>
> —Alexis de Tocqueville

Pontiac
Michigan

The Old Pontiac State Building, located on the corner of 28 North Saginaw and East Lawrence, and the city's tallest skyscraper, now occupies the place where the Yellow Tavern stood.

Today, Pontiac is home to 70,000 people. When Tocqueville and Beaumont arrived, it was a town with just twenty buildings and two inns. Following the Saginaw Trail, they made their way to Pontiac and stayed at the Yellow Tavern, which they were told was the town's premier inn. While he was here, Tocqueville interviewed tavern owner Amasa Bagley about frontier life.

Bagley was a large man Tocqueville described as, "... a man who, for fear of intimidating you, never looked you in the face while talking to you but waited, to consider you at his ease, until you were busy talking elsewhere." Tocqueville and Beaumont wanted to know how a pioneering family successfully cultivated land and handled illness. Also, they were curious about the role religion played in a frontier family's life. Bagley gave them a full account.

According to the innkeeper, land was cheap, but, because workers were in demand, labor was "beyond price." As for sickness, it was simple; there were no doctors. When a person fell ill, he or she either died or recovered.

Organized religion rarely reached the frontier, but when a preacher did make his way to the wilderness, all the area families came to hear him preach. Bagley told them, "It's in the wilderness that people show themselves almost starved for religion."

60

Old Pontiac State Building

Chiefly Pontiac

Pontiac was named for the great Ottawa Indian chief, Pontiac. In 1763, Chief Pontiac organized an unsuccessful resistance against the British at Fort Detroit. England was finally forced to relinquish control of Michigan in 1796—13 years after the Treaty of Paris and the end of the Revolutionary War.

In 1818-19, when Pontiac was founded, anti-British feeling was still intense. Local lore says that Pontiac's founders named the town after one of Britain's sworn enemies to rub salt in England's wound.

Ottawa Chieftain Pontiac

Finally, Tocqueville and Beaumont asked the tavern owner how to reach Saginaw. Tocqueville wrote later that their host's "...eyes dilated, his mouth opened," and that he cried, "You want to go to Saginaw!...to Saginaw Bay!...Have you thought that the woods are full of Indians and mosquitoes...Have you thought of the fever?"

But the two travelers had made up their minds. They had traveled this far and would not turn back. The next day as they set off for Saginaw, Tocqueville looked back to see the innkeeper still shaking his head and could hear him muttering, "I understand with difficulty what two foreigners are going to do at Saginaw."

What to See

Pine Grove

Located on the Saginaw Trail which led Tocqueville and Beaumont into the wilderness, this historic site was the home of a Michigan governor, Moses Wisner. Wisner acquired the estate in 1844, more than a decade after Tocqueville visited the area. Today the restored house, one-room school house, carriage house, smokehouse and farm museum are open for tours. Pine Grove is also the headquarters for the Oakland Historical Society. 405 Oakland Avenue. Tel: (248) 338-6732.

Oak Hill Cemetery

One of Michigan's oldest burial grounds, this picturesque cemetery stands on Pontiac's highest point. Many of Pontiac's founding citizens are buried here. Look for Stephen Mack's tombstone. Mack was the business manager of the Pontiac Company and a Revolutionary War patriot. At the foot of Governor Moses Wisner's grave, a bronze statue of a guardian angel stands. Legend says that Wisner dreamed of his guardian angel and later drew its image. After his death, his wife had the statue made from his drawing. 216 University Drive. Tours can be arranged through the Pontiac Historical Society. Tel: (248) 338-6732.

Pontiac
Today

Not much of the town Tocqueville and Beaumont described remains. The log cabins are gone and the stream has disappeared—replaced by a modern city.

In the 1880s, the Pontiac Spring Wagon Works began production, and the city hasn't stopped making vehicles since. Pontiac, still primarily a car town, is home to the Pontiac Division of General Motors. A rejuvenated downtown offers restaurants, shops and galleries. Be sure to visit the Creative Arts Center at 47 Williams Street. Tel: (248) 333-7849.

Inns and Outs

How to get there:
From Detroit take Highway 75 north, turn left on US 59 for 3 miles, and turn right onto Highway 24.

Where to stay:
For lodging information contact the Troy Chamber of Commerce. 4555 Investment Drive, Suite 300, Troy, MI 48098. Tel: (248) 641-8151.

Other Attractions

Meadow Brook Hall
For a look at how the auto barons of yesteryear lived, visit this 103-room, Tudor-style mansion. It was built by John Dodge in 1926 and contains everything from ornate bathrooms to a hidden staircase. Don't miss the gardens surrounding the house or the small playhouse, Knole Cottage, built especially for Dodge's daughter. Located at Oakland State University, 3 miles northeast from downtown Pontiac. Tel: (248) 370-3140.

Cranbrook Art and Science Museum
A 15-minute drive from Pontiac, this beautiful complex houses an art museum, a science center and a mansion. 1221 North Woodward Avenue. Tel: (248) 645-3323.

62

"... we finally caught sight of a clearing, two or three cabins and, what pleased us even more, a light. The river, which stretched like a violet thread at the end of the valley, convinced us that we had arrived in Flint River."

—Alexis de Tocqueville

Flint
Michigan

The two travelers made their way to Flint by way of the Saginaw Trail, passing through silent forests of tall trees and small silver lakes.

Tocqueville guessed that the wilderness was fleeting and that industry would make small settlements like the one at Flint River grow. He wrote in *Democracy in America* that "no people in the world have made such rapid progress in trade and manufactures as the Americans."

Flint is a perfect example. From building wagons to manufacturing cars, industry has always been at the city's core. General Motors, founded here in 1908, still employs approximately 70 percent of Flint's work force.

On July 25, 1831, the forest yielded surprises. Tocqueville and Beaumont met a man who was dressed in native garb. At first they thought he was a Native American, but, when he looked up, the Frenchmen recognized him as European. A pioneer, he lived alone in what Tocqueville described as a miserable log cabin. Tocqueville later wrote that the man was typical of settlers who "mingle love of savage life with the pride

The tavern where Tocqueville and Beaumont stayed was one of the first structures built in Flint and stood on the current site of the Riverfront Hotel at One Riverfront Center West.

Downtown Flint, circa 1890

of civilization and prefer the Indians to their compatriots, without however acknowledging them as equals." As the day wore on, Tocqueville and Beaumont hurried to reach Flint where they planned to spend the night.

The night grew dark and, with only the moonlight guiding them, Tocqueville and Beaumont crossed the river and reached the small settlement. Not yet a town, Flint was just a few small wooden buildings in the midst of the wilderness. One of these cabins was John Todd's tavern. Todd was among Flint's original settlers, and the area was later named Todd's Crossing. As they neared Todd's cabin, the moonlight revealed a big black bear, standing on its hind legs, chained to a fence. The Frenchmen were astonished. "What devilish country is this, where they have bears for watchdogs?" Tocqueville asked.

They shouted for their host. Eventually Todd came to his window and yelled at his bear to go to the kennel. The bear lumbered off and Tocqueville and Beaumont, exhausted, entered the cabin and found their beds.

What to See

Crossroads Village & Huckleberry Railroad

To discover more about life in the 1800s, visit this restored pioneer village with a sawmill, blacksmith shop, general store, printing press and church. Ride the Huckleberry Railroad, a Baldwin steam locomotive, and the *Genesee Belle,* a paddlewheel riverboat, which cruises around Lake Mott. Take I-475 to exit 13 and follow signs to G-6140 Bray Road, located in the Genesee Recreation Area. Tel: (810) 736-7100 or (800) 648-7275.

Genesee County Historical Society

The Historical Society offers programs throughout the year. PO Box 453, Flint, MI 48501. Tel: (810) 234-4225.

Alfred P. Sloan Museum

This museum houses everything from a 10,000-year-old mastodon skeleton to a Native-American wigwam. The Genesee County Gallery tells the story of Flint's early history with exhibits on

64 The *Genesee Belle*

Flint today

Native Americans and fur trading. The museum also showcases rare automobiles and documents the story of the automotive industry in Flint. The museum is located in the Flint Cultural Center on 1221 East Kearsley Street. Tel: (810) 760-1169.

Flint Today

Today, more than 140,000 people live in the city. The automotive industry remains as the core of the city's economic base.

Inns and Outs

How to get there:
From Detroit, take I-75 north to I-475 north and follow the signs to Flint.

Where to stay:
For lodging, contact the Flint Area Convention and Visitors Bureau.
519 South Saginaw Street, Flint, MI 48502.
Tel: (800) 25-FLINT or (800) 253-5468.

Other Attractions

Whaley Historical House
Dating to the 1850s, this 22-room Victorian mansion was owned by Robert J. Whaley. He loaned William Durant $2,000 to start the Flint Roadcart Company which grew into the Buick Motor Division, the first division of General Motors. 624 East Kearsley Street. Tel: (810) 235-6841.

The Flint Cultural Center
Flint's Cultural Center is located on tree-lined Kearsley Street and includes the Sloan Museum, Whiting Auditorium, Flint Institutes of Art and Music, the Flint Youth Theater and the Longway Planetarium. 1241 East Kearsley Street. Tel: (810) 760-1087.

Labor Museum & Learning Center of Michigan
This museum documents the division of labor in Flint's automotive industry and the impact of Michigan's labor movement on the country. 711 North Saginaw Street. Tel: (810) 341-1206.

65

Saginaw Michigan

The trip to Saginaw through the primeval forests was tough. Two young Indians led Tocqueville and Beaumont down the Saginaw Trail, past huge fallen trees and untamed vegetation. The Frenchmen were attacked by relentless mosquitoes and their provisions went bad.

As the day dwindled, their guides attempted to get them to stay the night in a deserted Indian village. But the Frenchmen wanted to spend the night in Saginaw where there was at least the prospect of supper and a bed. Tocqueville offered one of the Indian guides his water bottle as

incentive. The group pressed on, but soon their guides, who were on foot, became so exhausted that Tocqueville and Beaumont loaned them their horses.

The group traveled late into the night, until they reached a clearing beside a river. There an Indian canoe arrived to ferry them across the river to the small village of Saginaw. It was a sight that Tocqueville would remember for the rest of his life. The full moon rested on the horizon and in the pale light the canoe, "glided swiftly and without effort, long, narrow and black, like a Mississippi alligator making

A Beaumont drawing of the artist, Tocqueville and their guide

Saginaw, Michigan

66

The Forest for the Trees

Tocqueville knew the forests around Saginaw would disappear. He wrote, "In a few years, these impenetrable forests will have fallen, the noise of civilization and of industry will break the silence of the Saginaw." Chicago's Great Fire of 1871 helped fuel his prediction. After the fire, Saginaw's forests were felled to rebuild the windy city.

toward the bank to seize its prey."

The village stood on what is now the southern edge of Saginaw. Woods and a few farm pastures are there now. To picture where the old village was located, go to Wickes Park on 412 Wickes Park Drive and face the Saginaw River. Look southwest toward Green Point Island, and in the empty pastures across the river, imagine a few log cabins with about 30 inhabitants. This was the Saginaw that Tocqueville saw.

At that time, the small settlement consisted of a few French Canadians, Native Americans and what Tocqueville called "half breeds." While in Saginaw, he observed that even the majestic frontier was powerless in the face of human prejudice. He wrote that the small Saginaw community was divided: "The colour of their skin, poverty or wealth, ignorance or knowledge, have already established indestructible classifications among them; national prejudices, the prejudices of education and birth divide and isolate them."

The Castle Building

What to See

Green Point Environmental Learning Center

This 76-acre area lies on the flood plain of the Tittabawassee River, near to the old village where Tocqueville and Beaumont stayed. The center is a nice place to hike with over 120 species of birds living in the area. The learning center has exhibits on the area's natural wildlife. 3010 Maple Street. Tel: (517) 759-1669.

The Castle Museum of Saginaw County History

Once a federal post office, the museum's collections today showcase Saginaw history. It is also the headquarters for the Historical Society of Saginaw.
500 Federal Avenue.
Tel: (517) 752-2861.

The Castle Museum, a French-style chateau, was built as a result of a Federal Beautification Act in the 1890s. The act encouraged building design to reflect a region's heritage. Architect William Aiken built the Castle to honor Saginaw's French fur trading founders.

Shiawassee National Wildlife Refuge

To get a feel for Michigan's wildlife, visit the Shiawassee National Wildlife refuge. Four rivers meet at the refuge which is comprised of more than 9,000 acres. Close to 250 species of birds have been seen at the refuge. Tocqueville and Beaumont duck hunted near here, but today bird hunting (with the exception of limited goose hunting) is prohibited.

Saginaw Today

Today Saginaw County has a population of more than 200,000. Like many of the nearby cities, Saginaw is a car town. General Motors employs more than 14,000 people. Saginaw is also rich in parks—there are at least 30—and agriculture.

Inns and Outs

How to get there:

From Detroit, take Interstate 75 north to 46 west. From 46 west, follow the M13/ Washington Avenue. This road runs alongside the Saginaw River, and passes through the town.

Where to stay:

For hotel information contact the Saginaw County Chamber of Commerce.
901 South Washington Avenue, Saginaw, MI 48601.
Tel: (517) 752-7161. Or, contact the Saginaw County Convention and Visitors Bureau.
One Tuscola Street, Suite 101, Saginaw, MI 48607.
Tel: (800) 444-9979.

Other Attractions

Saginaw Art Museum

Housed in a Georgian-Revival mansion, surrounded by gardens designed by architect Charles Adams Platt, the art museum features everything from contemporary paintings and sculpture to 4,000-year-old Near Eastern ceramics. Look for exhibits from Michigan and Saginaw area artists. Children will enjoy the hands-on gallery where they can paint and work on ceramics.
1126 North Michigan Avenue.
Tel: (517) 754-2491.

Celebration Square

Surrounding Rust Park is Saginaw's Celebration Square which includes **Andersen Enrichment Center and Lucille E. Andersen Memorial Garden,** an educational, cultural and visitor's center.
120 Ezra Rust Drive.
Tel: (517) 759-1362.
Saginaw's sister city, Tokushima, Japan, helped raise funds for **The Japanese Cultural Center & Tea House.** Here you can experience a formal tea ceremony and wander through the gardens. Located on the corner of Ezra Rust Drive and South Washington Avenue.
Tel: (517) 759-1648.

Look for the C-SPAN plaque at the walkway entrance to the main building of the Green Point Nature Center.

68

> *"We arrived the second of August at Fort Gratiot[Port Huron], which is situated at the opening of Lake Huron at the beginning of the river St. Clair. Our arrival in this place was picturesque enough. It was evening: the sun had just gone down, stormy clouds covered the sky, lightning flashed on all sides."*
>
> —Gustave de Beaumont

Port Huron
Michigan

Situated on a sparkling blue waterway where the St. Clair River pours into Lake Huron, modern day Port Huron was once the site of Fort Gratiot. Tocqueville and Beaumont visited here in 1831, during the first days of August. When the two travelers arrived, there was little here but some wild marshes and a small fort. Fort Gratiot was hurriedly built at the close of the War of 1812 to protect the Lake Huron waterway from the British. In 1830, the fort guarded the Canadian/American border and was one of a network of American forts on the Michigan frontier.

Due to bad weather, Tocqueville and Beaumont were marooned for two days aboard a steamboat at Fort Gratiot. After having trekked through the Michigan wilderness, they reached Detroit and saw a notice advertising a steamship excursion into the vast waters of the Great Lakes.

Unable to resist one last venture into the American frontier, they signed on. Although they did not count on spending two precious days in Fort Gratiot, the Frenchmen made the best of it.

Tocqueville visited the fort and wrote briefly in his notebook, "Visit to the fort. Bearing of officers and soldiers. Drill. Insubordination." He also took his gun out for what he described as a "Good hunt in the swamp."

Today Port Huron residents continue to take advantage of the area's natural resources. Fishing and boating are popular in the summertime. At Pine Grove Park, fishing enthusiasts wield nets from the river bank. Both Pine Grove Park and Thomas Edison Park offer grand vistas of the area's waterways, and both are good locations from which to watch massive lake freighters and sail boats.

Fort Gratiot, which stood on the grounds of the present day Thomas Edison Inn at 500 Thomas Edison Parkway, has long since vanished.

Overview of Port Huron.

69

Water, Water, Everywhere

The Great Lakes contain six quadrillion gallons of water. If the Great Lakes were spread evenly over the continental United States, they would cover the entire country in close to nine and one half feet of water.

What to See

Fort Gratiot Lighthouse

Fort Gratiot Lighthouse, the oldest one in Michigan, has been guiding boats through the Blue Waterway since 1825. The lighthouse has been rebuilt and moved several times over the century. When Tocqueville and Beaumont visited, the lighthouse was located a few miles from the fort. An hour-long tour tells the history of the lighthouse. Tours are available Wednesday through Sunday, May 1st - October 1st.
Coast Guard Station, 2800 Omar Street.
Tel: (810) 982-3659.

> In the spring of 1996, the Coast Guard threatened to shut the Fort Gratiot Lighthouse down, but the community rallied to keep it operating.

Port Huron Museum

Native-American artifacts are showcased here along with a reconstructed Great Lakes freighter pilot house. All objects depict Port Huron's history. Decades after Tocqueville visited, Thomas Edison spent his boyhood in Port Huron. The museum has exhibits from Edison's boyhood laboratory and objects scavenged from Lake Huron shipwrecks.
1115 Sixth Street.
Tel: (810) 982-0891.

The Thomas Edison Depot of the Grand Trunk Railroad

Right next door to the Thomas Edison Inn is the depot which today acts as Port Huron's visitors center. It was here in 1859 that 12-year-old Thomas Edison boarded the train every day to sell concessions. He used his salary to buy supplies for a laboratory he built in the baggage car. You'll also find historical photos and exhibits of Port Huron. 95 Broadway.
Tel: (914) 941-3189.

The *Huron Lady* Cruise on the St. Clair River

Cruise down some of the same waterways which Tocqueville's steamship navigated on the *Huron Lady*, a 65-foot excursion boat. The tour takes you out past the lighthouse and along the St. Clair river. The *Huron Lady* leaves from a dock located at the Military Street entrance to

70   The Fort Gratiot Lighthouse

Blue Water Bridges

Michigan National Bank at 800 Military Street. Tours are not offered during winter months. Tel: (810) 984-1500.

Port Huron
Today

Today it is a city of more than 35,000, famous for its spectacular Blue Water Bridge which spans the river to Canada. Residents of Port Huron enjoy its waterways. In late July, thousands of people come to town for Mackinac Race Day, a sail boat race from Port Huron to Mackinac Island. Port Huron is the port for the St. Lawrence Seaway. On the other side of the Blue Water Bridge is the city of Sarnia, Ontario.

Inns and Outs

How to get there:
From Detroit, travel east on Interstate 94. Exit on business loop 69 and follow the signs toward downtown Port Huron.

Where to stay:
For lodging information call the St. Clair County Convention and Visitors Bureau. Tel: (800) 852-4242 or (810) 987-8687. Also try the Port Huron Chamber of Commerce. 920 Pine Grove Avenue, Port Huron, MI 48060. Tel: (810) 985-7101.

The C-SPAN plaque is temporarily located at Main Street Port Huron, a source for information about local events. 313 Huron Avenue. In 1999, it will be moved to the new Thomas Edison Museum, planned for the former site of Fort Gratiot, near the inn on Thomas Edison Parkway.

Port Huron, Michigan

71

"At 9 o'clock arrival at Sault-Sainte Marie. Delightful sight. Wonderful weather... Further on, two points of land covered with lovely trees, that shut the river in. Under the trees some wigwams. Between the points rapids."

—Alexis de Tocqueville

Sault Ste. Marie
Michigan

The Soo Locks, which raise and lower ships 21 feet between Lake Superior and Lake Huron in less than 15 minutes, are Sault Ste. Marie's main marvel. Today you can take a guided tour of the locks and climb an observation tower to see Canada.

The city gets its name from its patron saint, Mary or "Marie," and "sault," the French word for cascades.

When Tocqueville and Beaumont arrived aboard a steamship, the rapids of Sault Ste. Marie were not yet touched by man, and passage through the river was difficult. Bigger boats had to portage past the rapids. The Frenchmen sailed into Sault Ste. Marie with a party in full swing on the deck. Under the stars, Beaumont played an aria from Rossini's *Tancredi* on his flute.

At the time, Sault Ste. Marie was a remote trading outpost. To the outpost residents, the steamboat was still a wonder of modern technology. Tocqueville wrote, "At our arrival the whole population (stood) on the bank and on the roofs of houses.

Sault Ste. Marie's Fort Brady, 1830

Sault Ste. Marie, Michigan

A Sault Ste. Marie Love Story

John Johnston, one of Sault Ste. Marie's founders, came to the area in the 1790s as a fur trader. During a long winter, he became stranded in the snow and was rescued by an Indian chief and his family. While in their care, he fell in love with the chief's daughter, a princess named Woman of the Glade. Johnston asked her father for permission to marry her and was told he must wait one year. Johnston left vowing to return. The princess did not want to marry him until she had a dream in which a white man came to her, offering food and protection. She took this as a benevolent sign and the two were married. The couple had six children and built the town's first house.

A boat like ours (was) not seen more than once a year."

The population was a mix of Native Americans and fur traders, and they had a chance to talk to both. The day after their arrival Tocqueville and Beaumont rode the rapids in a canoe and visited an Indian traders camp where they spoke to the Johnstons, one of the founding families of Sault Ste. Marie.

They also visited Point aux Pins, now west of the city in Ontario, Canada, and met an Indian chief who gave Tocqueville the feathers from his headdress. It was a souvenir that Tocqueville treasured.

What to See

Soo Locks at Sault Ste. Marie

An average of 12,000 ships a year go through these locks which raise and lower ships between Lakes Superior and Huron. You can learn more about the locks at the **Visitors Center** through exhibits and a film on the history of the locks. Alongside the locks is the Soo Locks Park which is a good place to watch as the boats go through. Tours are available through **Soo Locks Boat Tours.**

Tel: (906) 632-6301. The **Soo Locks Train Tour** takes you 135 feet above the lock system as it crosses to Canada. At the Soo Locks train depot, you can take the **Haunted Depot Tour** where you "fall uphill" in a mystery bedroom, walk through a cemetery in a "storm," and explore a 60-foot underground tunnel. Tel: (800) 387-6200.

Tower of History

For a panoramic view of Sault Ste. Marie, climb or take the express elevator to the top of the Tower of History. From there you'll see a 1,200-mile scenic view of the river and Canada. The tower also displays local history exhibits.
501 East Water Street.
Tel: (906) 632-3658.

The Johnston House

This house, at the river's edge, belonged to the Johnstons, a founding family of Sault Ste. Marie. The house displays artifacts from the Historical Society's collection and is furnished with different period furniture and family keepsakes. Open only during the summer. Water Street. Tel: (906) 635-7082.

Look for C-SPAN's plaque in front of the Johnston House on Water Street.

Sault Ste. Marie's waterways

River of History Museum

Sault Ste. Marie was founded in 1668 when Father Jacques Marquette built the first mission church.

This museum traces the 8,000-year history of the St. Mary's River Valley with exhibits focusing on the first Native-American settlers, the French fur trade, and British and American expansion. The museum houses a complete replica of a French fur trader's cabin. 209 East Portage Avenue. Tel: (906) 632-1999.

Sault Ste. Marie
Today

The Sault Ste. Marie Tribe of Chippewa Native Americans makes its home here. The tribe is the city's biggest employer and runs the Kewadin Casino. More than 14,000 people live in the city. Its twin city, Sault Ste. Marie, Ontario, Canada, has a population of more than 80,000.

Inns and Outs

How to get there:
From Detroit, take I-75 north and take exit 392 or 394 to reach Sault Ste. Marie.

Where to stay:
For lodging contact the Sault Ste. Marie Convention and Visitors Bureau. 2581 on I-75 Business Spur, Sault Ste. Marie, MI 49783.
Tel: (800) 647-2858.

74

A boat passes through the Soo Locks

"Island three leagues round and fairly high. At the top the white defense-works of an American fort. On the shores some fifty houses, several of them rather pretty..."

—Alexis de Tocqueville

Mackinac Island
Michigan

Mackinac Island, with its charming summer cottages, car-free streets and many natural wonders is one of the few places that Tocqueville might still recognize. The Arch Rock, a natural granite formation, has not changed in the century and a half since Tocqueville first climbed it. Tourists still explore the caves that honeycomb the island and wonder at Sugar Loaf, a granite pyramid that stands 75 feet high.

Beaumont wrote, "This small island is the most picturesque thing I have yet seen in this region." He was so impressed with Arch Rock that he spent his day in Mackinac sketching it.

On August 7, 1831, Tocqueville wandered down to Mackinac Village and stopped by the home of Madame La Framboise. In 1830, she was one of Mackinac's most notable figures. After her husband's death, she took over his fur trading business and grew to be well-respected by both villagers and Native Americans. She was the great granddaughter of an Ottawa chief and her home became a meeting place, not only for fur traders but also for writers, poets and politicians. When Tocqueville visited, Madame La Framboise showed him a letter from a young Native-American woman and gave him a book of Indian prayers.

What to See

Colonial Michilimackinac

On the mainland, southeast of Mackinac Island, lies Colonial Michilimackinac where costumed guides take you through a reconstructed colonial fur trading village and military outpost. Visitors can be guests at a reenactment of an 18th-century French wedding, or watch archaeologists working on the nation's longest ongoing dig. Colonial Michilimackinac houses 18 authentic buildings on their original sites and includes Native-American programs and craft demonstrations. Exit 339 to Mackinaw City, at the southeastern end of the Mackinac Bridge. Tel: (616) 436-5564.

Madame La Framboise's home, now the Harbour View Inn, still boasts of Tocqueville's visit.

Beaumont's drawing of Arch Rock

The Sun Still Rises

Mackinac's famous Arch Rock has a Native-American legend attached to it. According to lore, there was once an Ottawa chief who committed such a shameful act that the Master of Life sent a furious wind to blow over the earth. The hills trembled, the waters roared and the sun fell from the sky, straight through Arch Rock. Legend goes on to say that no member of the Ottawa tribe ever again dared walk over Arch Rock.

Skull Cave

The C-SPAN plaque marking Tocqueville's journey is on Market Street, in front of the Stuart House.

Mackinac Island State Park

About 1,780 acres make up the park. Unusual geological formations such as Arch Rock and Sugar Loaf, as well as a scenic shoreline and trails, are all located inside the park. Beaumont and Tocqueville climbed Arch Rock and explored Sugar Loaf rock. About Sugar Loaf, Beaumont wrote, "In the rock are crevasses and faults where the Indians sometimes deposed the bones of the dead. I found a small fragment of these relics, and it's one of the riches that I shall bring back to my country."
Tel: (906) 847-3328
(May through September);
Tel: (517) 373-4296
(October through April).

Grand Hotel

The Grand Hotel

Built in 1887, the Grand Hotel speaks of elegant times past. Men are still required to wear ties and jackets and women must wear dresses. For a fee, visitors can walk through the Victorian gardens, or sit on the porch and take in the Straits of Mackinac. Guests can dance to a seven-piece swing orchestra, or let loose with a jazz band in the Cupola Bar. The hotel also offers a golf course, tennis, a wine bar and afternoon tea.
Tel: (800) 33-GRAND for information or reservations.

Indian Dormitory

The Indian Dormitory was the center where Native Americans came to receive annuities from the United States government. Today the museum explores how the 1836 Treaty of Washington affected Native Americans. Under the treaty, the Ojibwa and Odawa bands from Michigan's peninsula and the eastern half of the upper peninsula sold 15 million acres of land to the federal government in return for the right to remain in Michigan. Huron Street.
Tel: (906) 847-3328
(May through September);
Tel: (517) 373-4296
(October through April).

The Biddle House

While they were in Detroit, Tocqueville and Beaumont talked to Michigan Land Registrar John Biddle about the frontier. John Biddle's family built a clapboard house on Mackinac Island in the late 1700s. Today, guides in period dress take you back in time and show visitors how to weave, quilt and make candles. Market Street.
Tel: (906) 847-3328
(May through September);
Tel: (517) 373-4296
(October through April).

Mackinac Island

Fort Mackinac

Fort Mackinac

Set high upon the bluffs, historic Fort Mackinac provides a view of 19th-century military life. Costumed interpreters lead tours through the fort's 14 original historic buildings. The fort offers daily rifle and cannon demonstrations where you can help load and fire a cannon. The Tea Room at Fort Mackinac serves lunch and offers spectacular views of Mackinac Bridge, Lake Michigan and Lake Huron. Tel: (906) 847-3328 (May through September); Tel: (517) 373-4296 (October through April).

Inns *and* Outs

How to get there:
Cars are prohibited on Mackinac. Four ferry services that take you to the island leave from Mackinaw City or St. Ignace: the Arnold Transit Company at (906) 847-3351; Shepler's Mackinac Island Ferry at (616) 436-5023; Star Line Mackinac Ferry at (616) 436-5954 or (800) 638-9892. Great Lakes Air also provides flights. Tel: (906) 643-7165. For information on bicycle rentals on the island, contact the Mackinac Island Chamber of Commerce. Tel: (800) 454-5227.

Where to stay:
For lodging information call the Mackinac Island Chamber of Commerce. PO Box 451, Mackinac Island, MI 49757. Tel: (800) 454-5227.

William Beaumont, no relation to Tocqueville's traveling companion, was a Fort Mackinac surgeon who is credited with discovering the principles of human digestion. On June 6, 1822, a gun accidentally went off and shot 19-year-old Alexis St. Martin in the stomach. Beaumont operated and, although St. Martin recovered, an opening remained which led directly to his stomach. For more than a decade, Beaumont was able to examine St. Martin's digestive process. Beaumont published his results in 1833 and received world acclaim. St. Martin, Doctor Beaumont's patient, lived to the ripe old age of 78 and fathered many children.

> *"Arrival at 8 o'clock in the morning at Green Bay. Fort. Village on the bank in the middle of a prairie on the bank of a stream. Indian Iroquois village higher up. Large settlement."*
>
> —Alexis de Tocqueville

Green Bay
Wisconsin

Green Bay is passionate about its football team. The town is nicknamed "Titletown U.S.A.," a reference to the numerous Super Bowl championships won by the city's beloved Green Bay Packers.

The Packers are owned by share-holding citizens and run by a group of community leaders. All home games are sold out, and there is a 25-year waiting list for season tickets. Green Bay, a city of 100,000 people, is the third largest in the state.

Beaumont most likely visited with the Oneida Indians whose descendents now have a reservation and casino on Green Bay's west side. The Oneida reservation's casino is the city's biggest employer.

When Tocqueville and Beaumont arrived by steamship on August 9, 1831, Green Bay was a small frontier outpost just beginning to stir. Along the shore, there were only a few Indian villages and Fort Howard, which had been built in 1816 to defend America's interest in the Northwest.

Beaumont spent his time visiting an Indian village. He went from hut to hut conversing, sometimes in French, sometimes through gestures. He used his artistic talents to face-paint children and "learned the ways of the Indians better in half a day thus passed in their midst than I should have done in reading thousands of volumes."

Beaumont's sketch of Fort Howard

Tocqueville spent the day hunting. Beaumont wrote that Tocqueville "nearly drowned himself. He is very shortsighted; he encounters a stream and thinks it very narrow; he therefore does not hesitate to swim across. But he had been mistaken, and this river was actually so wide that he was utterly worn out when he reached the other bank."

Tocqueville downplayed the incident and wrote, "River crossed by swimming. Canoe, plants in the depths of the water. I lose myself a moment, return to the same spot without suspecting it."

Tocqueville and Beaumont also found time to interview a Fort Howard major about the future of Indians. The response was bleak. The officer told the Frenchmen that the Native Americans would not "bend themselves to civilization…they feared work, despised the comforts of the white man, and were too proud to change."

The travelers left Green Bay on August 10th and headed southeast to Detroit. The Green Bay visit marked the Frenchmen's last encounter with America's frontier.

What to See

Neville Public Museum
This museum is devoted to Green Bay history, science and art. *The Edge of the Inland Sea* exhibit travels back 12,000 years and traces Green Bay to the present. The museum also focuses on art and science. The *Whodunit* exhibit is a fun way to learn more about the science of solving crimes.
210 Museum Place.
Tel: (920) 448-4460.

Green Bay Packer Hall of Fame
You can throw a pass or kick the game-winning field goal at this museum devoted to the Green Bay Packers. The museum traces the history of the Packers from their start in 1919 as Curly Lambeau's Acme Packers to the present day team. The museum features seven video theaters, multi-media exhibits and the Super Bowl I trophy.
855 Lombardi Avenue.
Tel: (920) 499-4281.

Oneida Nation Museum
The largest exhibit of Oneida history and artifacts in the world is housed here. Hands-on exhibits allow visitors to touch baskets, cornhusk dolls, pipes and moccasins. Seven miles southwest of Green Bay on E and EE Streets.
Tel: (920) 869-2768.

A member of the Oneida tribe

Fort Howard

Heritage Hill State Park

Green Bay has a 40-acre outdoor museum devoted to its history. Costumed interpreters such as a French fur trader or a soldier relate tales about the times in which they lived and their life stories. The park has four sections to feature distinct historic periods: **La Baye** tells the early story of Green Bay and depicts the life of Jesuit missionaries and French fur traders; **Fort Howard** details the fort in 1836, five years after Tocqueville's visit; **Small Town** includes several original buildings of homes and businesses in 1871, a town hall, a firehouse and church; and the **Belgian Farm** includes a 1905 cheese factory. 2640 South Webster Avenue. Tel: (800) 721-5150.

Look for the C-SPAN plaque behind the Neville Public Museum at 210 Museum Place.

Green Bay
Today

Green Bay is famous not only for its football team but also for its production of cheese and dairy products. Papermaking is another large industry and the city is home to eleven mills. Green Bay, with its 24-foot deep channel, is an important domestic and international port.

Inns *and* Outs

How to get there:
From Milwaukee take 41 north to Green Bay.

Where to stay:
For lodging and hotel information, contact the Green Bay Area Visitors and Convention Bureau. 1901 South Oneida Street, Green Bay, WI 54307. Tel: (920) 494-9507.

Other Attractions

National Railroad Museum

Trains, trains, and more trains are housed here. More than 75 locomotive and railroad cars, including General Eisenhower's WWII Command Train, are on exhibit. 2285 South Broadway. Tel: (920) 435-7245.

NEW (North Eastern Wisconsin) Zoo

African lions, Australian wallabies, bald eagles and snow macaques reside at the NEW Zoo. Animals live in natural habitats. 4378 Reforestation Road. Tel: (920) 434-6814.

80

> *"There reigns in this place a profound and terrifying obscurity, now and again relieved by a flicker of light. Then you see the whole river, seemingly descending on your head. It is difficult to describe the impression produced by this ray of light, when, having let you a moment glimpse the vast chaos which surrounds you, it abandons you again amidst the darkness and fracas of the cataract."*
>
> —Alexis de Tocqueville

Niagara Falls
New York

Sun reflects off the mist and throws rainbows across the great Niagara gorge. The roar of the water, falling close to 200 feet, deafens visitors' ears. Native Americans aptly named the falls "Niagara" which means "thunder of the waters."

Niagara Falls is one of America's great wonders and is among the nation's oldest tourist attractions. The falls, bordered by Ontario, Canada and Niagara, New York, are made up of three cascades named the American Falls, Bridal Veil Falls and Horseshoe Falls. From November through January, during the Festival of Lights, the falls are illuminated with thousands of colored lights.

In 1831, when Tocqueville and Beaumont visited, the falls were untouched and unadorned. Tocqueville worried about the fate of the falls and wrote to a friend, "...if you wish to see this place in its grandeur, hasten. If you delay, your

> Look for the C-SPAN plaque at the entrance to Prospect Park in Niagara Falls.

Beaumont, Tocqueville and Miss Clemens viewing the Falls

A Barrel of Fun

For years, the falls have attracted daredevils. On October 24, 1901, 43-year-old Annie Taylor became the first person to go over Niagara Falls in a barrel. Encased in a padded oak drum, she went over the Horseshoe Falls at 4:23 p.m. and was pulled ashore 20 minutes later. She emerged from her barrel bruised and delirious but otherwise unharmed.

Niagara will have been spoiled for you. Already the forest round about is being cleared ... I don't give the Americans ten years to establish a saw or flour mill at the base of the cataract."

He was right. In the decade after Tocqueville's visit, mills, freight businesses and other manufacturers sprang up on the land surrounding the falls to take advantage of Niagara's water power. Private land owners catered to tourism and charged visitors money to look at the falls through a hole in a fence.

In the 1870s, Frederick Law Olmsted, a famous landscape architect, started a movement to bring the falls back to their natural state. In 1885, the land bordering the falls was bought by the state, and Niagara Reservation, a 400-acre park designed by Olmsted, was built.

In 1895, the Edward Dean Adams hydroelectric generating station opened in Niagara Falls and produced the newly-developed alternating current electricity, which allowed power to be transmitted long distances. The world was amazed when, one year after the station opened, it transmitted electricity to the city of Buffalo, 25 miles away.

Like most visitors to the falls, Tocqueville and Beaumont were awed by the spectacle of more than 750,000 gallons of water per second crashing over the gorge. The two men explored the falls from every angle, including a trip to the base. A hired guide took them under the falls where Tocqueville and Beaumont were

soaked by blinding spray and battered by strong winds. Back on top, the two men, along with two fellow tourists, Mr. Vigne and Miss Clemens, continued their exploration.

Beaumont made a sketch of the falls, but most of his time was spent trying to escape the attentions of Miss Clemens, a 40-year-old English woman who had taken a liking to him. Beaumont wrote that she was, "the best person on earth; but it is impossible to be more boring" and that "no power on earth could resist the will of Miss Clemens, and I suffered veritable violence ..."

It was with some relief that Tocqueville and Beaumont boarded a steamboat bound for Canada and left the powers of both Niagara Falls and Miss Clemens behind.

What to See

Niagara Power Project Visitors Center

Housed in one of the world's largest hydroelectric projects, the center tells the story of the falls and hydroelectric power. A platform allows access to salmon, trout, walleye and bass fishing. 5777 Lewiston Road, Lewiston. Tel: (716) 285-3211.

Whirlpool State Park

Tocqueville and Beaumont came here in 1831, probably on a hot

82

Horseshoe Falls

day in August, to escape from their unwanted travel companion, Miss Clemens.

Tocqueville described it as "a very picturesque site called the *Whirpull*." The park, with nature trails, is situated on a high bluff overlooking the whirlpool that is caused by the Niagara River's 90-degree turn. Located on the Robert Moses Parkway.

The Schoellkopf Geological Museum

Open from April through October, this museum explains the creation of the falls from the age of the great glaciers to the present day. Two miles north of Rainbow Bridge on the Robert Moses Parkway. Tel: (716) 278-1780.

Historic Lewiston

This is an 1820s historic village on the Niagara River with shopping and dining along the waterfront. Lewiston is home to **ArtPark** which presents a year-round season of plays, concerts and other events. PO Box 21, Lewiston, NY 14092. Tel: (716) 754-9500.

Tours of the Falls

You can explore the falls from top to bottom, by land and by water. The *Maid of the Mist* **Boat Tour,** which has been ferrying visitors around the base of the falls since 1846, is one way to experience the power of the billions of gallons of water that flow over the falls every hour. Tel: (716) 284-8897. The **Cave of the Winds Trip,** which is the modern day equivalent to Tocqueville's journey to the bottom of the falls, transports you by elevator 175 feet into Niagara Gorge to the base of Bridal Veil Falls. Tel: (716) 278-1730. The **New York State Park Viewmobile** offers a tram ride, stopping at points of interest throughout the falls. Tel: (716) 278-1730. Through **Niagara Historic Walking Tours,** you can learn the history of the falls on foot with a costumed interpreter as your guide. Seasonal operations. Call for an appointment. Tel: (716) 285-2132.

Maid of the Mist

The American Falls

Niagara Reservation State Park

This is the 400-acre park that Olmsted helped build in 1885 to preserve the majesty of the falls. The **Visitors' Center** in Prospect Park is a good place to start for an introduction to the falls and the surrounding parks. Tel: (716) 278-1796. The **New York State Park Observation Tower** at Prospect Point provides a dramatic view of all three falls. Tel: (716) 285-3893. **Goat Island,** located in the middle of the falls and rapids, has a footbridge that leads to the Three Sisters Islands and Luna Island, as well as the Rainbow Bridge which will take you to the Canadian side of the falls.

Niagara Today

Niagara, New York, with a population of approximately 60,000, is most famous for the falls. Tourism is the city's main industry, but hydroelectric and chemical companies are also headquartered here.

Luna Island

Inns and Outs

How to get there:
Take the New York State Thruway (I-90) to I-290 west which leads downtown. For a more scenic route, take I-90 to the Robert Moses Parkway and follow signs to the falls.

Where to stay:
For lodging information call the Niagara Falls Convention and Visitors Bureau. 310 Fourth Street, Niagara Falls, NY 14303. Tel: (800) 338-7890.

Other Attractions

Wintergarden

This glass-enclosed, seven-story botanical garden features tropical and desert plants plus trees and waterfalls. In downtown Niagara on Old Falls Street. Tel: (716) 285-8007.

Niagara's Wax Museum

The museum features life-sized wax figures in historic scenes. Niagara frontier memorabilia is also on exhibit. 303 Prospect Street. Tel: (716) 285-1271.

Daredevil Museum

This museum tells the stories of folks who went over and across the falls. 303 Rainbow Boulevard. Tel: (716) 282-4046.

84

"I can't express to you what pleasure we felt on finding ourselves in the midst of this population. We felt as if we were home, and everywhere we were received like compatriots, children of old France, as they say here. To my mind the epithet is badly chosen. Old France is in Canada; the new is with us ..."

—Alexis de Tocqueville

Montreal
Canada

In Montreal the past and the future mingle easily. Skyscrapers crowd downtown cosmopolitan avenues, while in Old Montreal, narrow winding streets and old buildings speak of bygone eras. Montreal is a busy port city filled with students from a number of colleges including McGill University and the University of Montreal.

When Tocqueville and Beaumont arrived by steamship on August 23, 1831, the city felt like a home away from home. They had been gone from their country for almost four months and were happy to speak their native tongue, to taste familiar foods and to understand local customs. Tocqueville was astonished to discover the size of the French settlement in Canada.

He wrote to a friend, "They are as French as you and I. They even resemble us more closely than the Americans of the United States resemble the English." Canada intrigued the two men. What was the relationship between the English and French settlers? Did the Canadians have the same freedoms as the citizens of the United States?

They met with a priest from the Saint-Sulpice Seminary and two young lawyers to gain some insight. They were told that Canadians enjoyed the same freedoms as Americans and while there was a little animosity between the French and English settlers, it did not "extend to the habitual intercourse of life."

However, they discovered that English settlers held the majority

1831 view of Montreal

85

Far East Farce

Like Christopher Columbus, Montreal's founder, Jacques Cartier, thought he had found the route to the Far East. He sailed up the St. Lawrence River in 1535, spotted the Island of Montreal but pressed on, certain that the Orient was just on the other side. However, he was stopped by fierce rapids and decided to go back and explore the island. He named the rapids La Chine in honor of China which he hoped lay just beyond them.

of the wealth, the trade and the influence in 19th-century Canada.

Tocqueville, ever the idealist, dreamed of a greater role for his compatriots. "I therefore still hope that the French, in spite of the conquest, will succeed some day in forming a fine empire in the New World, more enlightened, more moral, more happy than that of their fathers. For the present, this division between the two races is singularly favourable to the domination of the English."

Today, more than 160 years after Tocqueville's visit, the differences between French and English cultures continue as an issue of debate and have dominated Canadian politics for the last quarter century.

The Old Saint-Sulpice Seminary, dating back to the late 1600s, is still operating and stands on 130 Notre Dame West. Over the main doorway, look for the clock which dates from 1701 and is one of the oldest public timepieces in North America. The oldest building in Montreal, it is not open for tours.

What to See

Notre Dame Basilica (Basilique Notre-Dame)

This magnificent church, with its soaring blue vaulted ceilings ornamented with 24-carat gold stars, can hold 4,000 people. It was designed by James O'Donnell and built between 1824-29. Legend has it that O'Donnell was so inspired by his work that he converted to Catholicism after the church was completed. The basilica's organ is the largest in the world. In the back of the church, there is a small museum featuring paintings and historical artifacts.
110 Notre Dame West.
Tel: (514) 842-2925.

Maison de La Sauvegarde

Built in 1811 and among Montreal's oldest houses, this building is now a restaurant noted for its sausage sandwiches served on freshly baked bread—a delightful detour when touring Old Montreal. Chez Better Restaurant.
160 Notre Dame East.
Tel: (514) 872-9150.

Place Royale

The oldest public square in Montreal, Place Royale has been a market, a meeting place, a trading center and a public garden. Located at the corner of rue de la Commune and Place Royale.

86 Place Jacques-Cartier in Old Montreal

Old Port of Montreal (Vieux-Port de Montréal)

This is most likely the port where Tocqueville's steamboat docked. Because its docks are too small and its channels too narrow to handle modern freighters, the port has ceased to be the vital hub it once was. Old Port is now a popular park where Montreal's cyclists congregate. Visitors can board an excursion ship for a tour of the St. Lawrence River. 333 rue de la Commune West.

Youville Stables (Ecuries d'Youville)

These old stone buildings were warehouses when Tocqueville visited. Despite their name, they have never been stables. Today they are home to offices, shops and restaurants.
296-316 Place d'Youville.

Tourist Information Office (Office des Congrès et du Tourisme du Grand Montréal)

Once the site of the Silver Dollar Saloon, this small building is now a tourist information office. Built in 1811, the saloon got its name from the 350 silver dollars that were once nailed to the floor. 174 Notre Dame East.
Tel: (514) 844-5400.

Place Jacques-Cartier

This charming square with its cobblestone streets, horse-drawn carriages and flower stalls is a picturesque place to sip coffee in an outdoor café and watch the street artists and tourists walk past. Look for the statue of Horatio Nelson at the end of the plaza that was erected to commemorate Nelson's victory over Napoleon Bonaparte's troops. Bordered by rue de la Commune and Notre Dame East.

McCord Museum of Canadian History (Musée McCord)

Photographs, furniture, paintings, china and other objects document the last three centuries of life in Montreal. 690 rue Sherbrooke West.
Tel: (514) 398-7100.

Museum of Fine Arts (Musée des Beaux-Arts)

This museum contains the largest collection of paintings and sculptures from around the world with a focus on contemporary and Canadian art. The collection includes paintings by El Greco, Reynolds, Monet and sculptures by Rodin.
1379-1380 rue Sherbrooke West (at rue Crescent).
Tel: (514) 285-1600.

Parc du Mont-Royal

Montreal is named for this 761-foot-high hill. Jacques Cartier, Montreal's founder, dubbed it *Mont-Réal* (old French for "Royal Mountain"). Today it

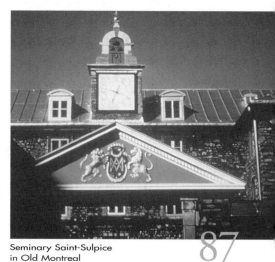

Seminary Saint-Sulpice in Old Montreal

is 494 acres of forest and paths.

The park was designed by famed landscape architect Frederick Olmsted. Sleigh rides are offered during winter months and both the Eastern Observatory (Obsérvatoire de l'est) and the Chalet du Mont-Royal offer spectacular views of Montreal and the St. Lawrence River. Tel: (514) 844-4928 for general information.

St. Joseph's Oratory (Oratoire St-Joseph), which perches high on a ridge of Mont-Royal, is one of the largest shrines in the world. It was built between 1924 and 1956 largely due to the efforts of Brother André, famous for his powers of healing. His heart is displayed in a glass case in the church's small museum. 3800 Queen Mary. Tel: (514) 733-8211.

In 1962, Montreal began building its underground city. This maze of passages, tunnels and plazas provides a subterranean network connecting two railroad stations, 1,600 boutiques, 1,700 businesses, two universities, countless stores and more. The city beneath the city is a warm place to retreat during cold winter days.

Montreal History Center (Centre d'Histoire de Montréal)

This red brick building was once the city's main fire house. Its exhibits and slide shows document the history of Montreal from the first Native Americans to present day. Most of the descriptions are in French but the museum has an English visitor's guide.
335 Place d'Youville, at rue St-Pierre. Tel: (514) 872-3207

Montreal Museum of Archaeology and History (Musée d'Archéologie Pointe-à-Callière)

This museum is actually built around the city's first ruins. A multi-media show sets the stage and introduces the city's rich history beginning with its founding in 1642. Visitors make their way through the remains of the century-old city where stone walls and passages are accented by spotlights and holographic figures. 350 Place Royale, on the corner of rue de la Commune. Tel: (514) 872-9150.

Montreal *Today*

Montreal is a city of tourists, universities, haute cuisine and businesses. Francophones, or French-speaking citizens, make up 66 percent of Montreal's population. The city's neighborhoods include downtown with its corporate headquarters and luxury hotels; Old Montreal with its historic buildings and winding streets; the Latin quarter with its bistros and cafés; Chinatown;

Museum of Montreal History

View of downtown from Montreal's Mont-Royal

and the impressive Parc du Mont-Royal, the city's "mountain" park that rises from the center of Montreal.

Inns *and* Outs

How to get there:
From New York City take I-87 north to connect with Canada's Autoroute 15 at the border and stay on the expressway for the entire 400-mile journey to Montreal. Be sure to bring proper identification for customs.

Where to stay:
For lodging call the Tourist Information Center (Centre Info-Touriste). The staff is bilingual. 1001 Square-Dorchester. Tel: (514) 873-2015 or (800) 363-7777.

Other Attractions

Just for Laughs Museum (Musée Juste Pour Rire)
Opened on April Fool's Day in 1993, this museum is dedicated to the art of laughter. Exhibits include film clips of the world's most famous clowns and gifted comics. The museum also features a 250-seat cabaret where hopeful amateurs can try out their routines.
2111 Boulevard St-Laurent. Tel: (514) 845-4000.

Biodôme de Montréal
The Biodôme houses four unique ecosystems. Visitors can wander through an Amazon rain forest complete with monkeys and parrots; a forest with live birch and maple trees, otters and fish; an Antarctic with live penguins and puffins; and see some of the wildlife of the St. Lawrence River.
4777 Avenue Pierre-de-Coubertin. Tel: (514) 868-3000.

Botanical Garden (Jardin Botanique)
The gardens encompass 180 acres, including a Japanese garden with an art gallery, a tearoom where ancient tea ceremonies are performed, an insectarium and, in the summer months, an outdoor aviary where butterflies congregate.
4101 rue Sherbrooke East. Tel: (514) 872-1400.

> *"... the river is magnificent. Quebec is on a very picturesque site, surrounded by a rich and fertile countryside. Never in Europe have I seen a more lively picture than that presented by the surroundings of Quebec."*
>
> —Alexis de Tocqueville

Quebec City
Canada

Time has pretty much stood still in the walled city of Old Quebec. The same gabled houses and magnificent vistas exist today that Tocqueville and Beaumont saw during their visit in late August 1831. Perched high on Cape Diamond and below on the banks of the St. Lawrence River, Quebec City is divided into upper and lower sections that are connected by steep streets, staircases and two public elevators.

Upper town, or Old Quebec, is where you can find most of the city's well-preserved historic stone buildings including the Citadel, built to stand guard over the port and the city, and the Ursuline Convent, founded in 1639.

Struck by the natural beauty of the city and the surrounding countryside, Tocqueville and Beaumont spent their days exploring the area. They traveled to nearby Montmorency Falls and wandered the Plains of Abraham where, in 1759, the British seized control of Quebec City from the French. Beaumont took out his sketchbook and captured the falls and the view of the St. Lawrence from the ramparts.

"But what has interested us most keenly in Canada," Tocqueville wrote, "are its inhabitants." The two travelers felt at home with the French Canadians; they shared the same sense of humor and customs.

Quebec City gets its name from the Algonquian Indians who called the city "Kebec," meaning "where the river narrows." The city is situated at the narrowest point of the St. Lawrence River, near its outlet into the Gulf of St. Lawrence.

90

Beaumont's sketch of the St. Lawrence River from Quebec City

Quebec City, Canada

A gateway to Old Quebec

"They are still Frenchmen, trait for trait... Like us, they are animated, alert, intelligent, apt to scoff and easily carried away, great talkers and very hard to control when their passions are fired," wrote Tocqueville.

The pair talked with villagers, interviewed statesmen, visited a Quebec courtroom and read the French newspapers in an attempt to learn more about the French Canadians. Tocqueville and Beaumont noted that, despite the wide stretch of frontier that spread out to the Pacific Ocean, the French Canadians, unlike the Americans, were not rushing to settle new lands. "The Canadian is tenderly attached to the soil which saw him born, to his church, to his family. That is why it is so hard to get him to go seek his fortune elsewhere," wrote Tocqueville.

But while the two travelers praised the values of the French Canadians, they worried about the Canadians' fate. When Tocqueville and Beaumont arrived in Quebec City, it was teeming with British soldiers busy putting the finishing touches on the Citadel, which was completed in 1832. It seemed to the two Frenchmen that the wealthy English occupied the most powerful positions and controlled the money. Tocqueville wrote, "They already feel clearly that the English race is encircling them [the French Canadians] in an alarming manner..."

The visiting Frenchmen thought that if the French Canadians could gain their independence, they might have a chance of forming a new French society, a society made up of people "more moral, more hospitable, more religious than in France." Far away from the troubled politics of their homeland, Tocqueville and Beaumont saw a chance for a new French beginning.

It was a dream that Tocqueville would reluctantly abandon. After interviewing citizens and talking to officials, Tocqueville concluded that it would not happen. On leaving Quebec City, aboard a steamship headed back to the United States, Tocqueville wrote, "The odds are therefore that Lower Canada will end by becoming a people entirely French. But it will never be a numerous people. Everything around them will become English. They will be a drop of water in the ocean."

Old Quebec is the only walled city in North America north of Mexico.

What to See

Museum of Civilization (Musée de la Civilisation)

The story of Quebec City unfolds in this dramatic glass museum through hands-on displays, holograms, videos and other creative exhibits. There is a display of Old Quebec houses in miniature as well as exhibits featuring furnishings and artifacts from fur trading days to present day. 85 rue Dalhousie. Tel: (418) 643-2158.

> Outside Quebec City, Montmorency Falls rise 274 feet, 100 feet higher than Niagara Falls.

Montmorency Falls

Located seven miles from Quebec City, the waterfall, which Tocqueville and Beaumont explored, is surrounded by a park. Even in winter the falls are awe-inspiring. The frozen spray builds a mountain of snow and ice at the base of the falls called Sugarloaf. Visitors can tour the falls by cable car and a footbridge that spans the falls. A tourist information office is located at the falls parking entrance. Tel: (418) 663-2877.

Place Royale

Tocqueville and Beaumont would have recognized the Normandy-style architecture of the houses in this square. Near the banks of the river in lower town, the square was once the center of town. Due to threats of attack, villagers moved to the top of the cliff. When Tocqueville and Beaumont arrived, the square was a center for shipbuilding and logging. An information center about the square is open from June through September. 215 rue du Marché-Finlay. Tel: (418) 646-3167.

Museum of French America (Musée de l'Amérique Française)

Located in Quebec City's historic seminary, which was founded in 1663, this museum is devoted to exploring French culture in North America. The collection includes European and Canadian still lifes and landscapes dating back to the 15th century; rare colonial coins; books; parchments; and movies that tell the story of French culture in Canada. 9 rue de l'Université. Tel: (418) 692-2843.

Explore Sound and Light Show

In a theater shaped like an early sailboat complete with rigging, visitors can watch a multi-media show about the Age of Exploration with stories of Columbus, Vespucci, Cartier and Champlain. 63 rue Dalhousie. Tel: (418) 692-2063.

Beaumont's sketch of Montmorency Falls

92

Fortifications that once protected Quebec City

Fort Museum (Musée du Fort)

Using a sound and light show as well as a 400-square-foot model of the city, this museum recreates the six sieges on Quebec City, including the Battle of the Plains of Abraham. 10 rue Ste-Anne. Tel: (418) 692-1759.

Battlefields Park (Parc des Champs-de-Bataille)

More than 250 acres of parkland, including the grassy Plains of Abraham, make up this famous city retreat. In nice weather the park abounds with bikers and joggers and is the frequent site of outdoor concerts. Open year round, the Interpretation Center provides guided tours around the Plains of Abraham. Avenue Wolfe-Montcalm. Tel: (418) 648-5641.

Ursuline Museum (Musée des Ursulines)

During his visit to Quebec City, Tocqueville wrote "...the convents of women have useful aims and give examples of charity regarded with lively admiration by the English themselves." He was likely referring to the Ursuline Convent, founded in 1642 and the oldest school for women in North America. Today visitors can explore the convent's chapel and museum which contains samples of golden embroidery woven by the Ursulines. Other artifacts include the skull of General Montcalm, the French commander who lost Quebec City to the British in the Battle of the Plains of Abraham. 12 rue Donnacona. Tel: (418) 694-0694.

Old Port of Quebec (Vieux-Port de Québec)

Tocqueville and Beaumont's steamship most likely anchored at this port which dates back to the 17th century. At one time, it was one of the busiest ports in the world. **Port de Quebec in the 19th Century,** an exhibition center, chronicles its history. 100 rue St-André. Tel: (418) 648-3300.

Quebec City

Quebec City *Today*

Quebec City is the capital of Quebec province. Its skyline is dominated by Quebec City's most famous hotel, Château Frontenac, which was modeled after the great châteaus of France's Loire Valley. With its old-world charm and unique location, Quebec City is one of North America's top tourist attractions. Horse-drawn carriages are a picturesque way to explore the city. In February, Quebec City is known for its Winter Carnival where snow sculptors congregate and the nights are highlighted by parades. The city has a population of approximately 600,000, 95 percent of whom are French-speaking. The city is also home to biotechnology, manufacturing and logging firms.

Inns *and* Outs

How to get there:
From New York City take I-87 north to connect with Canada's Autoroute 15 to Montreal. From there pick up Autoroute 20 and follow to Quebec City.

Where to stay:
For lodging and tourist information, call the Greater Quebec Area Tourism and Convention Bureau. 835 avenue Wilfrid-Laurier, Quebec, Canada G1R2L3. Tel: (418) 649-2608. The Quebec Government's Tourism Department also operates an office at 12 rue Ste-Anne. For more information contact Tourism Quebec. PO Box 979, Montreal, Quebec H3C2W3. Tel: (800) 363-7777.

Other Attractions

Quebec Museum (Musée du Québec)
This museum contains eight galleries of art which focus on works from Quebec artists. 1 avenue Wolfe-Montcalm. Tel: (418) 643-2150.

Augustine Museum (Musée des Augustines de l'Hôtel-Dieu de Québec)
The museum's collection includes artifacts from Quebec City's earliest days including paintings, furniture, silver and antique medical instruments. It is located at the convent of the Augustine Sisters who founded the first hospital in North America in 1639. 32 rue Charlevoix. Tel: (418) 692-2492.

94

> *"We were struck by the appearance of riches and prosperity reigning in Massachusetts; everything there proclaims a happy population; it is no longer that wild nature that one meets with everywhere in the states of the west; the virgin forest has long since disappeared and you no longer find a single trace of it."*
>
> —Gustave de Beaumont

Whitehall
New York & Stockbridge
Massachusetts

Stockbridge's Main Street, made famous in a painting by native artist Norman Rockwell, is quintessential New England. The town remains much the same way it looked when Tocqueville and Beaumont visited on September 8, 1831. The cobblestone sidewalks, historic homes and the fire-engine-red Congregational Church, which Beaumont sketched, have stood virtually untouched for over 160 years.

Tocqueville and Beaumont traveled by steamship from Quebec City down the St. Lawrence River to Lake Champlain. They disembarked in Whitehall, New York, a small town at the lake's southernmost tip.

From Whitehall, they headed overland to Stockbridge in western Massachusetts, intent on meeting Catharine Maria Sedgwick, a celebrated American author whose books had been translated into several languages. She was just one of the contemporary American writers who resided in Stockbridge.

Tocqueville and Beaumont never did meet Catharine

Nathaniel Hawthorne wrote *The House of Seven Gables* in Stockbridge, not long after the Frenchmen returned to Europe.

Whitehall Bay in 1830

Sedgwick Pie

The Sedgwick family is buried in the village cemetery in a circular pattern. Judge Theodore Sedgwick's tombstone, a high obelisk, is placed in the center of the circle. All other family tombstones radiate around it. Locals have dubbed the burial site Sedgwick Pie. The only non-Sedgwick to be buried in the pie is Elizabeth Freeman (Mum Bet) who was freed from slavery under Massachusetts' law. Theodore Sedgwick was her lawyer. Today members of the Sedgwick family still live in the family home on Main Street. Modern-day film star Kyra Sedgwick is a member of the Sedgwick clan.

Sedgwick house, 1830

Sedgwick; she was out of town. They did, however, meet Catharine's nephew Theodore III. Later stationed in Paris as an attaché for the U.S. government, Theodore assisted Tocqueville in writing *Democracy in America*.

What to See

Skenesborough Museum in Whitehall, New York

The museum houses a sixteen-foot diorama complete with a light and sound show that details how the Navy was built. The museum also contains a diverse collection of toys, tools and railroad artifacts. Skenesborough Drive, Box 238, Whitehall, NY.
Tel: (518) 499-0716.

Mission House

Built in 1739 by Reverend John Sergeant, the first missionary to the Mahican Indians, the Mission House offers visitors a glimpse of Stockbridge during colonial times. The house is filled with authentic colonial

furnishings and exhibits about the town's evolution. There is also a small Native-American museum and colonial flower garden.
19 Main Street, Stockbridge, MA.
Tel: (413) 298-3239.

Chesterwood

Chesterwood is the summer estate of Daniel Chester French, the sculptor best known for the Lincoln Memorial in Washington, DC. Visitors can tour his studio and see a collection of more than 5,000 works.
4 Williamsville Road, Stockbridge, MA.
Tel: (413) 298-3579.

Norman Rockwell Museum

One of Stockbridge's most famous residents was Norman Rockwell. A museum dedicated to his art is situated on 36 acres and surrounded by the picturesque Berkshire Hills. Visitors can tour his studio (open May through October) and view the largest collection of Rockwell's work in the world.
Route 183, Stockbridge, MA.
Tel: (413) 298-4100.

Naumkeag

In the late 1800s, wealthy East Coast families discovered the beauty of the Berkshire Hills. Stockbridge has a number of "cottages" or summer mansions built during the Gilded Age. Naumkeag, built in 1885 for the Choate family, is one of the few mansions open to the public. A guided tour takes you through the opulent house. Be sure to stroll through the stately gardens. Open Memorial Day through Columbus Day.
5 Prospect Hill Road, Stockbridge, MA.
Tel: (413) 298-3239.

Whitehall & Stockbridge *Today*

Whitehall is a small town of approximately 4,400 people located along the shores of Lake Champlain. It is known as the birthplace of the U.S. Navy and, in the summer of 1776, 13 ships were built in its modest harbor to counter a British invasion. They became the basic corps of

Stockbridge Main Street at Christmas by Norman Rockwell

Whitehall, New York's historic business district.

the American fleet.

Stockbridge is a picturesque town in all seasons. Many artists and writers have made the town their home.

The Stockbridge Library has almost five shelves devoted to works by hometown authors including Edith Wharton, whose family home stands in nearby Lenox.

The Berkshire Hills and Stockbridge Bowl, a 1.5-mile-long by one-mile-wide lake, make Stockbridge a favorite vacation spot. In the summer, Tanglewood, a concert arena for world famous musicians, plays host to the Boston Pops, symphony orchestras and other ensembles.

Beaumont's sketch of the
Congregational Church in Stockbridge

Inns and *Outs*

How to get there:

To reach Whitehall, New York from I-87, take exit 20. Turn left on NY Route 149, go 13 miles and then travel north on US Route 4, 11 miles to Whitehall.

To reach Stockbridge from I-87, take exit 17 and follow I-84 to the Taconic State Parkway north to Route 23 east. Follow the signs to Stockbridge.

Where to stay:

For lodging in Whitehall, contact the Whitehall Chamber of Commerce. 259 Broadway Drive, Whitehall, NY 12887.
Tel: (518) 499-2292. For lodging information in Stockbridge, contact the Stockbridge Chamber of Commerce. 6 Elm Street, Stockbridge, MA 01263.
Tel: (413) 298-5200.

Other Attractions

Berkshire Botanical Gardens

Fifteen acres of landscaped gardens and a woodland walk provide visitors a scenic respite. At the intersection of Routes 183 and 102, Stockbridge, MA.
Tel: (413) 298-3926.

98

> *"It is without contradiction the most interesting city that we have seen up to the present. We are exerting every effort to penetrate to the bottom of things, and I think we shall succeed. We see people of all kinds, of all nationalities, and of diametrically-opposed opinions."*
>
> —Gustave de Beaumont

Boston
Massachusetts

Boston—the hub of New England—is a state capitol, college town, a major financial center and one of the country's most historic cities. A walk along the wharves of the Charlestown Navy Yard gives visitors a spectacular view of the harbor. It is around this harbor that the first sparks of the American Revolution were ignited in 1773 when a group of angry colonists protested English taxes by dumping tea into the harbor.

Over the course of three centuries, Boston has welcomed thousands of immigrants to the United States. In the 18th century, many Puritan settlers arrived and took advantage of the city's prosperous shipping center to become wealthy merchants. Those moneyed merchants formed a tight uppercrust society known as the Boston Brahmins.

It was this closed society that Tocqueville and Beaumont butted against when they first arrived in Boston on September 9, 1831. "...the first day we were not happy in our attempts; we were unable to accost anyone. We found ourselves in an embarrassing position, because we had no letters of introduction for Boston," wrote Beaumont. It was a hard first few days. Tocqueville had received devastating news. His childhood tutor, a friend whom

Tocqueville loved, had died. "In that moment I experienced... the keenest and most poignant grief that I have ever felt in my life."

Tocqueville soon had many engagements to distract him from his grief, for Boston society, having learned more about the two aristocrats, opened its doors. "There is not a minute of our time unoccupied; we are pursued by invitations; we hardly ever dine at our hotel, and almost every evening we have a ball, or a political meeting." At these outings, the two nobles met some of the nation's most prominent men, including the famous Senator Daniel Webster and former President John Quincy Adams.

Portrait of John Quincy Adams

Molasses Flood

On January 15, 1919, a large storage tank in Boston's North End exploded. It contained millions of gallons of molasses. An actual wall of molasses, estimated to be 15-30 feet high, flowed into the streets. Some of the victims caught in the flow path were suffocated, cooked alive and swept into the harbor. Twenty-one people were killed and more than 100 were injured. The molasses flood caused millions of dollars worth of damage and took more than six months to clean up. Boston Harbor was temporarily stained brown; the cause of the explosion was never determined.

Tocqueville seized the opportunity to discover more about the fledgling democratic country. He asked Charles Curtis, the legal solicitor for the city of Boston, to outline the American jury system. He asked John Quincy Adams about freedom. Adams told him, "... we live in freedom, and know nothing else! Massachusetts was nearly as free before the revolution as to-day. We have put the name of the people where was the name of the king ..."

Tocqueville also interviewed Jared Sparks, a well-known editor, about the system of America's town government. The simple, natural process of the self-governing town impressed the French noble. This became a key point, which Tocqueville discussed in *Democracy in America*. "In the township, as well as everywhere else, the people are the source of power; but nowhere do they exercise their power more immediately. In America the people form a master who must be obeyed to the utmost limits of possibility."

*S*What to *See*

The Old North Church

Built in 1723, this colonial church made history the night of Paul Revere's famous ride. On April 18, 1775, Robert Newman, the Church's sexton, climbed the steeple and hung two lanterns to signal that the British were coming by sea. 193 Salem Street. Call to arrange tours. Tel: (617) 523-6676.

Paul Revere Statue and Old North Church

Paul Revere House

Located in Boston's North End, this is the oldest house in Boston (circa 1680) and was once the residence of Paul Revere, America's legendary Revolutionary War messenger. Visitors can tour the house to gain a sense of a typical colonial home.
19 North Square.
Tel: (617) 523-1676.

Faneuil Hall and Quincy Market

This historic structure was erected in 1742 to serve as a meeting hall and a public market. Within these walls, slavery, women's rights, and almost every American war have been debated. Tocqueville and Beaumont attended a rally supporting Polish Independence here on September 12, 1831. Beaumont wrote, "On entering the Hall we saw an immense gallery entirely filled with very well-dressed ladies, without admixture of any man. In almost all public meetings in the United States, this separation of men and women takes place." Behind the hall is Quincy Market with outdoor cafes, street performers and shopping.
Bordered by Clinton, Chatham and Commercial Streets.
Tel: (617) 523-1300.

USS Constitution

Nicknamed "Old Ironsides," this warship has an amazing record of winning 42 battles against powerful men-o'-war from the British Fleet during the War of 1812. She got her nickname because British cannonballs are said to have bounced off the vessel. Launched in Boston in 1797, the ship is the oldest commissioned warship afloat in the world. Visitors can tour the ship and the *USS Constitution* Museum to learn more about the ship's history. Charlestown Navy Yard.
Tel: (617) 426-1812.

Isabella Stewart Gardner Museum

Friend to some of the exceptional artists of her time, including painter John Singer Sargent and novelist Edith Wharton, heiress Isabella Stewart Gardner collected an impressive array of art. Today her Venetian-style mansion includes 2,000 works of art, including master paintings, sculptures, furniture and art.
280 The Fenway.
Tel: (617) 566-1401.

Boston Tea Party Ship and Museum

On the *Beaver II,* a replica of a Boston Tea Party Ship, visitors are invited to tour the ship, wear Indian headgear and dunk a trunk of tea into the harbor. Closed December through February.
Congress Street Bridge.
Tel: (617) 338-1773.

Boston Common

Colonists used to graze cows on Boston Common, the oldest public park in the United States. Today it is a beautifully landscaped park that's often the site of festivals and political rallies.
Bordered by Beacon, Park, Tremont, Boylston and Arlington Streets.

Follow the brick or red painted line marking Boston's Freedom Trail. The route winds its way past many historical buildings associated with the Revolutionary War. Freedom Trail Rangers conduct walking tours and are ready to answer questions. Start the trail at the Boston National Historical Park Visitors Center at 15 State Street.
Tel: (617) 242-5642.

101

Harrison Gray Otis House

Harrison Gray Otis, a well-respected lawyer, congressman and former mayor of Boston, was famous for his hospitality. He invited Tocqueville and Beaumont to dine at his mansion on Beacon Hill. This Federal-style mansion, designed by Charles Bulfinch and built in 1796, was Otis' first residence. Today the house is operated by the Society for the Preservation of New England Antiquities and is open for tours. 141 Cambridge Street. Tel: (617) 227-3956.

Boston's oldest neighborhood, the North End is home to some of the best Italian restaurants on the East Coast. Many wine shops, gourmet markets and bakeries are also located here.

Granary Burying Ground

Many of Boston's famous, early citizens are buried here, including Samuel Adams, John Hancock, Paul Revere and several signers of the Declaration of Independence. Corner of Tremont and Bromfield Streets.

The State House

Visitors can't miss the gold top dome of the State House which is situated at the top of the Common. Designed by Charles Bulfinch in 1798, it is the seat of the state government. The marble interior is hung with paintings chronicling Boston's rich history. Open for tours. Beacon Street between Joy and Bowdoin Streets. Tel: (617) 727-3676.

Black Heritage Trail

In the 19th century, the city's African-American population lived on the north slope of Beacon Hill. This trail passes historic sites, including the **African Meeting House,** the oldest African-American church in the United States. It was here that the New England Anti-Slavery Society was formed a year after Tocqueville and Beaumont visited. 46 Joy Street. Tel: (617) 742-1854. Tours of the **Black Heritage Trail** can be arranged through the National Park Service. Tel: (617) 742-5415.

Commonwealth Museum

Next door to the John F. Kennedy Museum, this museum traces the history of the Commonwealth of Massachusetts with exhibits on Native Americans, immigrants and natural history. 220 Morrissey Boulevard. Tel: (617) 727-9268.

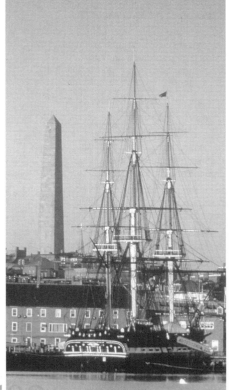

102

USS Constitution and Bunker Hill Monument

Charles River boathouse and skyline

Boston
Today

From Beacon Hill, with its red brick society mansions, to the colorful streets of Chinatown, Boston is a city of distinct neighborhoods. Visitors can explore the trendy Back Bay area with its old Victorian houses, the Irish South End, the Italian North End and Newbury Street, the city's poshest shopping district.

Boston is also a center of higher education—Boston College and Boston University are two of the many colleges situated within city limits. Across the river in Cambridge is Harvard University, the nation's oldest institution of higher learning. The largest city in New England, Boston has a population of more than six million.

Inns and Outs

How to get there:
From the north or south, take I-95 to I-93. Follow I-93 to downtown Boston. From the west, take I-90 into the city.

Where to stay:
For lodging and tourist

information contact the Greater Boston Convention and Visitors Bureau. 2 Copley Place, Suite 105, Boston, MA 02116. Tel: (617) 536-4100.

Other Attractions

Museum of Fine Arts
An extensive collection of art including Asian collections and European works from the 11th through the 20th century. 465 Huntington Avenue. Tel: (617) 267-9300.

Museum of Science
Visitors can watch lightning being made, explore microscopic life and watch a re-creation of gems growing underneath the Earth's surface in this extensive science museum. Science Park. Tel: (617) 723-2500.

John F. Kennedy Library and Museum
Designed by I.M. Pei, this museum is a memorial to JFK and contains historical documents and films on the Kennedys' life. Columbia Point, off Morrissey Boulevard. Tel: (617) 929-4500.

The C-SPAN plaque, marking Tocqueville's journey, is located in the Boston Public Library, near Copley Square. 700 Boylston Street.

Hartford
Connecticut

Perched on a hill in the center of Hartford is the gold-domed state capitol building. From here, visitors look out over a revitalized downtown area. Home to insurance companies and the high tech industry, this capital city's roots go deep into American history; in 1662, Hartford's town leaders drew up a charter of independence.

The Hartford Asylum for the Deaf and Dumb, which stood on 139 North Main Street in West Hartford, is now the site of the American School for the Deaf.

The city, on the banks of the Connecticut River, soon developed into a thriving commercial center. When Tocqueville and Beaumont visited in the fall of 1831, Hartford was a center of banking and trade. It was also the site of the famed Hartford Asylum for the Education of the Deaf and Dumb.

Tocqueville and Beaumont stopped in to visit the asylum. There they met Julia Brace, a young woman who could not see, hear or speak. "From time to time she smiled at her thoughts. It was a singular spectacle. How can the ridiculous or the amusing appear to a spirit thus immured, what form does it take?" wondered Tocqueville.

He wasn't the only one who was curious. Fourteen years later, Doctor Samuel Howe received permission to take Brace from the asylum and enroll her in an institute in an attempt to teach her to read. Brace never learned to read, but she became the first deaf and blind person in America to receive instruction.

104

The Old State House in Hartford, circa 1840

The Charter Oak

In 1662, the colony of Connecticut was granted a charter by King Charles II allowing it considerable autonomy. Twenty-five years later, Governor Edmund Andros demanded that the colony give up its charter. He traveled to a Hartford inn to retrieve it, but after the document was laid out on the table, the candles were extinguished and it disappeared. Captain Wadsworth of Hartford is said to have seized the charter and hidden it in a nearby oak tree. The tree stood until August, 1856 when a storm uprooted it. Today a monument stands on Charter Oak Avenue, marking the place where the historic tree once stood.

What to See

Museum of Connecticut History, Connecticut State Library

This museum houses the charter of 1662. The wooden frame, encasing the charter, is made from the famous oak tree. There is also an exhibit on Colonel Samuel Colt's firearms, which were first manufactured in Hartford. The library features history, law and social science sources, a genealogy collection and state archives.
231 Capitol Avenue.
Tel: (860) 236-5621.

Bushnell Park

Located next to the State Capitol, the 41-acre park contains more than 600 trees and features the Soldiers and Sailors Memorial Arch, a 116-foot-high memorial dedicated to Hartford citizens who served in the Civil War. The park features a restored 1914 carousel with intricately hand-carved horses, chariots, mirrors and 800 lights.
Downtown Hartford.
Tel: (860) 246-7739.

Wadsworth Atheneum

Founded in 1842 by Daniel Wadsworth, this is the oldest public art museum in the nation. The 50,000-object collection spans over 5,000 years and includes paintings, textiles, bronzes, Native-American art and J.P. Morgan's collection of early American silver. The museum also features the largest collection of Hudson River School landscape paintings in the country. 600 Main Street.
Tel: (860) 278-2670.

Christ Church Cathedral

Built in 1828, this is one of America's oldest Gothic-style churches. 45 Church Street.
Tel: (860) 527-7231.

Connecticut Historical Society

The society has nine galleries devoted to exhibits on the state's history. The society also features a research library housing 100,000 books and manuscripts. 1 Elizabeth Street.
Tel: (860) 236-5621.

Old State House

When Tocqueville and Beaumont visited, this building was the state capitol. It housed the Connecticut Legislature from 1796 to 1878 and was designed by Charles Bulfinch, who later designed the national capitol.

105

The Old State House has a series of exhibits including the rather bizarre **Joseph Steward's Museum of Oddities** which displays, among other things, a two-headed cow, a two-headed pig and a collection of fossils. 800 Main Street. Tel: (860) 522-6766.

State Capitol

Guided tours of the gold-domed capitol building are available to the public. 210 Capitol Avenue. Tel: (860) 240-0222.

Hartford
Today

The capital of Connecticut, Hartford has taken advantage of its location on the Connecticut River to emerge as a major industrial center. Hartford has a population of approximately 140,000 and is known as the "Insurance City" because it is the headquarters for many insurance companies such as Aetna and Travelers. Its newspaper, *The Hartford Courant,* claims to be the oldest continually operating paper in the nation.

Inns *and* Outs

How to get there:
To reach the greater Hartford area in the center of the state, follow Interstate 84 east/west or Interstate 91 north/south to downtown.

Where to stay:
For lodging and tourist information, contact the Greater Hartford Convention and Visitors Bureau. One Civic Center Plaza, Hartford, CT 06103. E-mail: GHCVB@connix.com. Tel: (860) 728-6789 or (800) 446-7811. Also try the Greater Hartford Tourism District. 234 Murphy Road, Hartford, CT 06114. E-mail: ctfuntour@aol.com. Tel: (860) 244-8181 or (800) 793-4480.

State Capitol building

Soldiers and Sailors Memorial Arch in downtown Hartford

Other Attractions

Mark Twain House

Within these walls, Samuel Clemens, better known as Mark Twain, wrote *Huckleberry Finn, The Adventures of Tom Sawyer,* and *A Connecticut Yankee in King Arthur's Court.* The house was built in 1874 and Mark Twain lived there with his wife and daughter until 1891. Guides lead visitors through the house which has period furnishings and an interior designed by Louis Tiffany. 351 Farmington Avenue. Tel: (860) 247-0998.

Sightseeing Tours

Deep River Navigation Company offers visitors an opportunity to see Hartford from the Connecticut River. Tel: (860) 526-4954.
The Hartford Guides offer walking tours through Hartford's historic neighborhoods. Tel: (860) 522-0855.
Heritage Trails Sightseeing also offers city tours. Tel: (860) 677-8867.

Harriet Beecher Stowe House

The home of Harriet Beecher Stowe, author of *Uncle Tom's Cabin,* contains Stowe's original furnishings, including the author's writing table. 73 Forest Street. Tel: (860) 525-9317.

Butler-McCook Homestead

Built in 1782, the homestead is the oldest home in Hartford and was occupied by the Butler-McCook family for four generations. 396 Main Street. Tel: (860) 522-1806.

Look for the C-SPAN plaque at the east courtyard entrance of the Old State House in downtown Hartford.

107

Wethersfield
Connecticut

A walk down Wethersfield's Main Street is a walk through time. Situated along the Connecticut River, the town has the state's largest concentration of historic houses. Stately residences dating back to the 18th century line quaint, gas-lanterned streets. Many of Wethersfield's old homes are open for tours, including the red brick Webb House, built in 1752. During their stay in Wethersfield, Tocqueville and Beaumont dined here with prison commissioner Judge Martin Welles.

While in Wethersfield, Tocqueville and Beaumont dined at the Webb House. Here, Count Rochambeau and George Washington devised plans that led to a colonial victory at Yorktown.

The pair arrived here in early October of 1831 to tour the new Connecticut State Prison. It was not a visit they eagerly anticipated. "There is there a famous prison [in Wethersfield], which we absolutely must examine; and though we should prefer to busy ourselves with something other than the Penitentiary System, we yet do not want to neglect our duty," wrote Beaumont.

Due to its productive prison labor force, the penitentiary became one of the few in the nation that actually paid for itself. The two Frenchmen were also impressed by the limited amount of corporal punishment prison officials used. However, behind this positive picture, controversy was brewing.

Three years after their visit, allegations of misconduct emerged. The prison warden was accused of stealing food supplies, forcing sick prisoners to work and making prisoners drink foul water. The Frenchmen did not witness those abuses, but Tocqueville was skeptical about the ability of American prisons to reform convicts. In a letter to his father, he wrote, "...the American system is more economical than ours...the men subjected to it never

Carving from Wethersfield's
Ancient Burial Ground

Wethersfield's Colonial Meeting House and Congregational United Church of Christ

become worse in the prisons than they were on entering. But do they really reform themselves? ...What's certain is that I would never confide my purse to those honest people."

What to See

Webb-Deane-Stevens Museum

Located on Wethersfield's historic Main Street, the museum complex features three restored 18th-century homes, including the Webb House which was owned by Judge Welles. Today, visitors can tour the three houses which feature furniture and artifacts from 1660 to 1840. Open May through October. 211 Main Street. Tel: (860) 529-0612.

First Church of Christ, Congregational United Church of Christ

The church, established in 1635, has also served as a town meeting hall since 1761. It is one of only three colonial meeting houses left in New England. The town's oldest burial grounds are located behind the church. 250 Main Street. Tel: (860) 529-1575.

Cove Warehouse

Between 1650 and 1830, Wethersfield's maritime trade flourished. The Cove Warehouse features exhibits on the town's once-great shipping industry and the pirates that made their living scavenging the trading fleet. The warehouse also tells the story of Wethersfield's illustrious onion trade. North end of Main Street. Tel: (860) 529-7656.

The Cove Warehouse

Wethersfield Museum

Once a public school, the museum is housed in the Keeney Memorial Cultural Center and features regional artifacts, period furniture, portraits and paintings. Beginning in the spring of 1998, an exhibit entitled *Legendary People, Ordinary Lives* will chronicle Wethersfield's outstanding citizens. 200 Main Street. Tel: (860) 529-7161.

The red onion was developed in Wethersfield during the 1750s as a product to barter with Native-American traders from the West. Small, specially designed ships were built locally to transport the onions to coastal markets.

Wethersfield
Today

Wethersfield, with a population of 26,000, lies just ten minutes by car south of the capital city of Hartford. The restored central area of the town, highlighted by the Congregational Church, retains its colonial feel despite the fact that much of the town lies along busy Interstate 91.

Inns and Outs

How to get there:
Follow Interstate 91 north/south to Wethersfield.

Where to stay:
For lodging and tourist information contact the Greater Hartford Convention and Visitors Bureau. One Civic Center Plaza, Hartford, CT 06103. E-mail: GHCVB@connix.com. Tel: (860) 728-6789 or (800) 446-7811. Also try the Greater Hartford Tourism District. 234 Murphy Road, Hartford, CT 06114. E-mail: ctfuntour@aol.com. Tel: (860) 244-8181 or (800) 793-4480.

Other Attractions

Sightseeing Tours
Deep River Navigation Company offers visitors an opportunity to see sites along the Connecticut River. Tel: (860) 526-4954.

Dinosaur State Park
Ten minutes south of Wethersfield is a 63-acre park with thousands of preserved dinosaur tracks dating back to the Jurassic Period. The exhibit center showcases dinosaur skeletons. West Street, Rocky Hill. Tel: (860) 529-8423.

110 *Red Onions by Margret Lloyd*

> *"Philadelphia is an immense city... All the houses are of brick... following the English custom, and the streets are straight as string."*
>
> —Alexis de Tocqueville

Philadelphia
Pennsylvania

Within a single square mile in Philadelphia, you can visit the cradle of American independence. The hall where the first Constitutional Convention convened, the site of Benjamin Franklin's house and the Liberty Bell all stand in the historic center of Philadelphia.

In the city where the U.S. Constitution was crafted, Tocqueville set out to investigate the principles of a democratic republic. He and Beaumont arrived in town on October 12, 1831 and booked a room at the elite Mansion House hotel. They stayed in town for more than a month during a spectacular fall. "...the sky [was] pure and sparkling as on the most beautiful summer days...All the shades of

[foliage] red and green are mingled together; this is really the moment when America appears in all her glory," Tocqueville wrote to his mother.

The Frenchmen's days in Philadelphia were filled with "...Prisons, learned societies, and salon gatherings in the evening: there's our life." The two men visited Eastern State Penitentiary, a sprawling, castle-like fortress that was the pride of the Pennsylvania System.

Opened in 1829, the prison was based on the Quaker principles of reform—solitary imprisonment, religious

Tocqueville and Beaumont's hotel, the Mansion House, which was located on South 3rd Street in the Society Hill neighborhood, was destroyed in a fire in 1847.

Mansion House on South 3rd Street

111

For Whom the Bell Tolls

In 1752, the Liberty Bell was commissioned by the Pennsylvania Assembly. After arriving from London, the bell cracked the first time it was struck. Despite its crack, the bell continued to be rung for a number of years to announce important occasions. The bell pealed when the Constitution was ratified and at the inauguration of John Adams. The bell also tolled at the deaths of George Washington, Benjamin Franklin, Alexander Hamilton, John Adams and Thomas Jefferson.

instruction and hard work. It was at Eastern State Penitentiary that Tocqueville, for the first time, gained the prisoners' perspectives. Armed with a pencil and a notebook, Tocqueville entered the inmates' cells and questioned them about solitary confinement, prison conditions and their work. He discovered that most inmates preferred the new prison system to the old where convicts were thrown together in a common cell.

Tocqueville also took advantage of Philadelphia society to continue investigating different perspectives of American democracy. Through formal dinners, dances and

On 5th Street, alongside Independence Square, stands Philosophical Hall. Tocqueville and Beaumont visited here and met with many members. Founded in 1743 by Benjamin Franklin, the American Philosophical Society is the oldest learned society in America. Not open to the public.

evenings spent at the American Philosophical Society of Philadelphia, Tocqueville and Beaumont met most of the city's leading citizens. Tocqueville asked Nicholas Biddle, president of the Bank of the United States, about political parties. He spoke with Henry D. Gilpin, who would later become the Attorney General of the United States, about the American jury system. And he interviewed Charles Jared Ingersoll, a former candidate for Vice President of the United States, about political associations. Tocqueville was laying the groundwork for *Democracy in America*. From Philadelphia, he wrote to his father, "It seems to me that I have some good ideas [about the United States], but I don't yet know in what framework I will place them..."

What to See

Society Hill
This old Philadelphia neighborhood has changed little since Tocqueville and Beaumont stayed here. Today Society Hill consists of quaint red brick shops, restaurants and houses set along narrow cobblestone streets. On 127-129 Spruce Street, **A Man Full of Trouble Tavern Museum** features tours of the 1757 tavern lead by costumed guides. Tel: (215) 922-4367.

112   The Liberty Bell

The Powel House, home of Samuel Powel, the last colonial mayor, is also open for tours. 244 South 3rd Street. Tel: (215) 627-0364.

Despite its name, **Society Hill** is not situated on a hill. The area is named for the Free Society of Traders who received a land boon from William Penn in the 17th century. Society Hill stretches between Walnut and Lombard Streets and South 2nd and South 5th Streets.

Independence National Historic Park

Known as "America's most historic square mile," the park includes many of the sites where the nation was born. **The Visitors Center** provides maps, a film and exhibits focusing on America's colonial period. The Second Continental Congress convened in **Independence Hall**. America's leaders met in the hall to hammer out the Constitution. Prior to that, the Articles of Confederation were drafted here. Chestnut Street between 5th and 6th Streets.

Declaration House is a reconstructed house where Thomas Jefferson rented rooms and wrote the Declaration of Independence. Exhibits include a film and displays on the history of the house. Corner of 7th and Market Streets. The **Liberty Bell** is housed in a glass encasement. Park rangers tell legends and facts about the bell that was last rung on Washington's birthday in 1846. Market Street, between 5th and 6th Streets.

A tribute to Benjamin Franklin, **Franklin Court** includes a steel structure which outlines the site of the colonial statesman's house. There is an underground museum offering displays, interactive exhibits and a brief film on Franklin's life. Adjacent to the steel-framed house, visitors will find renovated buildings which contain an 18th-century printing office, an archaeological exhibit and a postal museum. Market Street, between 3rd and 4th Streets.

Carpenters' Hall is the site of the First Continental Congress which convened here in 1774. 320 Chestnut Street. The **City Tavern,** still an operating restaurant, is a reconstructed colonial tavern. While writing the Declaration of Independence, Thomas Jefferson stopped here for a few drinks. 2nd and Walnut Streets. **Congress Hall** served as the meeting place for the U.S. Congress from 1790 to 1800 when Philadelphia was the nation's capital. Corner of 6th and Chestnut Streets. Call for more information on Independence Park attractions. Tel: (215) 597-8787.

Independence Hall

Philadelphia Museum of Art along Schuykill River

Philadelphia Museum of Art

Ranked as one of America's premier art institutions, the museum houses more than 300,000 pieces including early Quaker and Amish art as well as Shaker crafts. The collection features masterpieces by Paul Cézanne, Vincent Van Gogh, Claude Monet and Nicolas Poussin. Visitors can also see a reconstruction of a 12th-century French cloister and a 16th-century Indian temple. *Rocky* film fans may recall that Sylvester Stallone made his victorious run up the steps of this museum. Today visitors can see snap-happy tourists reenacting Rocky's triumphant run.
26th Street and Benjamin Franklin Parkway.
Tel: (215) 763-8100.

Elfreth's Alley

The city's oldest residential street was once the neighborhood of artisans such as blacksmith Jeremiah Elfreth. The **Mantua Maker's Museum House** provides information on the street's homes and past residents. North of Arch Street, between Front and 2nd Streets.
Tel: (215) 574-0560.

Arch Street Friends Meeting House

This is the oldest Quaker Meeting House still in use in America. It was built in 1804 near Quaker burial grounds. Guides answer questions about the history of the Quakers and their meeting house. Quaker artifacts are on display. Every spring, the Philadelphia Yearly Meeting of Friends is held here.
320 Arch Street, between 3rd and 4th Streets.
Tel: (215) 627-2667.

Eastern State Penitentiary

"Gigantic walls, crenellated towers, a vast gate of iron give to this prison the aspect of a vast chateaufort of medieval times," is the way Tocqueville and Beaumont described Eastern State Penitentiary. Today the prison is a museum where

Eastern State Penitentiary, 1831

Benjamin Franklin Parkway in downtown Philadelphia

visitors can tour cell blocks, death row and the high-walled solitary yards where prisoners once kept gardens and exercised. Al Capone was once incarcerated here.
22nd Street and Fairmount Avenue.
Tel: (215) 236-3300.

Rodin Museum

This museum contains one of the largest collections of Rodin's pieces. The museum showcases 124 pieces of the sculptor's work. Benjamin Franklin Parkway at 22nd Street.
Tel: (215) 763-8100.

Franklin Institute Science Museum

Erected in honor of Benjamin Franklin, the museum has hands-on exhibits and demonstrations relating to many fields of scientific exploration including physics, computers, mathematics and astronomy. 222 North 20th Street and Benjamin Franklin Parkway. Tel: (215) 448-1200.

Academy of Natural Sciences

America's first museum of natural history features an excellent dinosaur exhibit. 1900 Benjamin Franklin Parkway. Tel: (215) 299-1000.

Philadelphia
Today

In a few spots, such as Society Hill and Independence Square, Philadelphia still looks much as it did during colonial times. But the city also has a modern heart with office buildings that serve as headquarters for many corporations. Philadelphia, with its population of approximately 1.5 million, is the nation's fifth largest city. Visitors can explore the city's ethnic neighborhoods and its theater and museum districts. It is also a college town with Drexel University, the University of Pennsylvania and Temple University all located here.

Inns and Outs

How to get there:

From the south, follow I-95 north to I-676, which will take you into the center of the city. From the north, follow the New Jersey Turnpike to Camden/Philadelphia (exit 4). Take the Benjamin Franklin Bridge and follow to Vine Street which leads into the city.

Where to stay:

For lodging information contact the Philadelphia Convention and Visitors Bureau. 16th Street and John F. Kennedy Blvd.
Tel: (800) 537-7676 or (215) 636-1666.

Other Attractions

Atwater Kent Museum

This small museum has thousands of objects from Philadelphia's past plus exhibits on archaeological explorations and the history of the city.
15 South 7th Street.
Tel: (215) 922-3031.

Betsy Ross House

In America's most famed seamstress' house, visitors can learn about the history of the American flag and gain insight into colonial life. The house features Ross' personal possessions and furnishings.
239 Arch Street.
Tel: (215) 627-5343.

Penn's Landing

The place where William Penn first landed in 1682 is now a waterfront park area and home to three historic ships. Built in 1883, the *Gazela* was once a Portuguese fishing boat. The *U.S.S. Olympia,* built in 1892, was the flagship of the North Atlantic Squadron during the Spanish-American War. From the landing, visitors can get a clear view of Camden, New Jersey which lies across the Delaware River.

Philadelphia is derived from Greek words meaning "city of brotherly love."

Fairmount Park

Stretching across thousands of acres along the banks of the Schuykill River, Fairmount Park is the largest landscaped city park in the world. Meadows, rolling hills, playgrounds, trails and bicycle paths provide an idyllic retreat. The park contains the oldest zoo in the nation, a number of restored colonial mansions and Boathouse Row, which features a number of 19th-century boathouses. Accessible by Kelly Drive, West River Drive and Belmont Avenue.
Tel: (215) 685-0000.

Christ Church

This was the church where Benjamin Franklin, George Washington and Betsy Ross worshipped. The Georgian-style church was built in 1727. Its steeple stands 196 feet high and contains the font from which William Penn was baptized in 1644. The burial ground contains the graves of Benjamin Franklin and four other signers of the Declaration of Independence.
2nd and Market Streets.

City Hall

Standing in the center of Philadelphia, City Hall divides the city into North and South. A 37-foot bronze statue of William Penn stands at the top of the building. The tower provides a panoramic view of the city.
Broad and Market Streets.
Tel: (215) 686-2840.

U.S. Mint

The world's largest mint provides visitors with a look at the coin-making process.
5th and Arch Streets.
Tel: (215) 408-0114.

116

> *"We were charmed by those of Baltimore. The week that we spent in that city was a real carnival; we went from feast to banquet steadily."*
>
> —Gustave de Beaumont

Baltimore
Maryland

Baltimore today is a city of many cultures. From Little Italy to the streets of Greektown and Little Lithuania, the neighborhoods display the city's rich diversity. However, when Tocqueville and Beaumont arrived at the end of October in 1831, they encountered a distinctively Southern city. European immigrants had not yet made their mark in Baltimore. Society consisted of wealthy merchant families and a few landed gentry, who did their utmost to show the two Frenchmen a good time.

The two nobles attended a number of balls where the women, according to Tocqueville, were "remarkably pretty" though "dressed in bizarre fashion." Lavish dinner parties were thrown in their honor and the two men also attended the Baltimore Races which Beaumont called "a very fine horse race." Baltimore continues to be known for its horse racing; the Preakness, one of racing's Triple Crown events, is held here annually.

Despite the flurry of social events, Tocqueville and Beaumont's investigation of Baltimore took a serious turn. On their way to the races, the two travelers saw a black man assaulted for using a "white" entrance. The next day they visited an almshouse where they witnessed a black man who had been so abused by a slave trader that he had lost his mind. Tocqueville wrote, "he was lying on the floor rolled in a blanket which was his only covering. His eyes rolled in their sockets and his face expressed at the same time terror and fury. It was a horrible sight."

Beaumont later wrote *Marie*, a novel based in part on his observations in Baltimore. It was one of the first novels written decrying the evils of slavery and prejudice.

During his stay, Tocqueville asked John Latrobe, a distinguished Baltimore lawyer, if he thought Maryland could survive without slavery. Latrobe, a leader in the cause to repatriate African Americans to Liberia, told him that it was possible, and perhaps even economically advantageous to abolish slavery in Maryland. Latrobe went on to say, "... we often notice that freeing them [slaves]

> While in Baltimore, Tocqueville and Beaumont met with Charles Carroll, the last living signer of The Declaration of Independence. The 95-year-old Carroll told them "a mere Democracy is but a mob."

Poe-ticulars

At the juncture of Battery Street and Key Highway, Federal Hill Park, once the site of a Civil War fort, provides a panoramic view of Baltimore's Inner Harbor and the city.

produces great troubles, and that the freed negro finds himself more unhappy, and more stripped of resources than when a slave." Tocqueville adopted this idea and wrote in *Democracy in America*,

"...independence is often felt by him to be a heavier burden than slavery..."

The Edgar Allan Poe House

What to See

Star Spangled Banner Flag House

During the War of 1812, Francis Scott Key stood on the deck of a warship anchored in Baltimore Harbor and watched as the British made an unsuccessful attempt to capture the city. Inspired by a tattered American flag that had withstood British fire, he wrote the "Star Spangled Banner."

This was the house of Mary Pickersgill, maker of the famous flag that inspired Francis Scott Key to write the work which became our national anthem. The 15-star, 15-stripe flag is now on display at the Smithsonian Museum in Washington, DC. The Pickersgill house contains Federal period furnishings and a collection of early American art. 844 East Pratt Street. Tel: (410) 837-1793.

The Baltimore Poe House and Museum

Edgar Allan Poe lived in this small row house from 1832-35 with his aunt and his cousin Virginia Clemm, whom he would later marry. A number of Poe's possessions are exhibited, including the lab desk that he used at the University of Virginia and the only known portrait of Poe's wife. A series of displays and videos relate Poe's life story. 203 Amity Street. Tel: (410) 396-7932.

Washington Monument and Museum at Mount Vernon

In his travel journal, Tocqueville wrote, "At Baltimore the Washington memorial, which is 160 feet high and cost, I think, a

118

The Pimlico Race Track

million francs, was erected partly by association." A 30-ton statue of George Washington sits atop the tall, white monument. More than 200 steps and a winding staircase bring visitors to the top where four windows provide a stunning view of the city. Elevators are not available. Mount Vernon Place at West Pratt and North Charles Streets.
Tel: (410) 396-0929.

B&O Railroad Museum
A mecca for train lovers, the B&O museum is a 37-acre indoor/outdoor collection of engines, locomotives and railroad cars dating back to 1829. Visitors enter the museum through the old Mount Clare Station off Poppleton Street at 901 West Pratt Street.
Tel: (410) 752-2490.

Fort McHenry National Monument and Historic Shrine
This star-shaped fort protected Baltimore from the British during the War of 1812. During the Civil War, Union forces used the fort as a prison camp for Confederate soldiers. It was a hospital for troops during World War I and a training center for the U.S. Coast Guard during World War II. In the restored barracks and visitor center, military memorabilia and historic interpretations are exhibited. End of East Fort Avenue.
Tel: (410) 962-4290 or (410) 962-4299 for group tours.

Basilica of the Assumption of the Blessed Virgin Mary (Baltimore Cathedral)
Designed by Benjamin Latrobe, the basilica is the oldest cathedral in the United States. Corner of Cathedral and Mulberry Streets.
Tel: (410) 727-3564.

Mount Clare Museum House
The Georgian-style mansion was home to the Carroll family and its patriarch Charles Carroll, whom Tocqueville and Beaumont met during their visit to Baltimore. The house includes original period furnishings. 1500 Washington Boulevard, Carroll Park.
Tel: (410) 837-3262.

Across the street from John Latrobe's house stands the neoclassical Baltimore Cathedral. It was designed in the early 1800s by Latrobe's father, Benjamin Henry Latrobe, one of America's premier architects. He also designed Statuary Hall, the Old Senate Chamber and the Old Supreme Court Chamber in the nation's capital.

A view of Baltimore from Federal Hill

Baltimore *Today*

With a population of more than 700,000, Baltimore is a thriving port city and fascinating place to explore. **Fells Point,** with its Federal-style buildings, is home to some of the city's oldest pubs. The city has seven enclosed markets, crowded with vendors selling everything from fresh shrimp and oysters to home-baked bread. **Oriole Park** at Camden Yards, the home of baseball's Baltimore Orioles, is a great place to watch a game. **Johns Hopkins University,** one of the preeminent universities in the country, is located in Baltimore. The city, located at the upper northern end of Chesapeake Bay, remains a major port for grain, coal and spices.

Inns and Outs

How to get there:
From Washington, DC, take 95 north to Baltimore. Exit 395 to downtown Baltimore. From the north, take 95 south and exit 395 to downtown Baltimore.

Where to stay:
For lodging information contact the Baltimore Area Convention and Visitors Association. 100 Light Street, 12th Floor, Baltimore, MD 21202. Tel: (410) 659-7300.

Other Attractions

National Aquarium in Baltimore
The Aquarium is one of the city's most popular attractions. A 265,000-gallon pool at the entrance of the aquarium contains small sharks, a hawksbill turtle and stingrays of every size, including a few albino ones. Other exhibits include *Surviving Through Adaptation,* which explores how animals adapt to their environment. Pier 3, 501 East Pratt Street. Tel: (410) 576-3800.

Baltimore Museum of Art
The museum contains a wide collection of European paintings, furnishings, silver and African art. The Cone Collection includes paintings by Picasso, Matisse, Van Gogh and other masters. 10 Art Museum Drive at North Charles and 31st Streets. Tel: (410) 396-7100.

Walters Art Gallery
In this gallery, you'll find an extensive collection of art including Faberge Eggs, tapestries, illuminated manuscripts and 19th-century paintings. 600 North Charles Street, off East Centre Street. Tel: (410) 547-9000.

120

"...we had arrived at Pittsburg[h], the most industrial town of Pennsylvania, the Birmingham of America, where the air is constantly obscured by the multitude of steam engines that run the shops."

—Gustave de Beaumont

Pittsburgh
Pennsylvania

Today numerous parks stretch alongside Pittsburgh's famous three rivers—the Allegheny, the Monongahela and the Ohio. Within and around city limits, fishermen cast their lines for bass. At night, the Boardwalk, along the banks of the Allegheny River, comes alive with jazz and a bustling restaurant scene. This lively riverfront activity has arisen in the last decades as Pittsburgh has redeveloped its waterfront. But for close to a century, the city was known for its heavy industry which created billowing smoke and polluted rivers. Situated between the three rivers and rich with limestone and coal deposits, Pittsburgh was destined by geography to become an industrial town. Taking advantage of Pittsburgh's natural resources, some of America's best-known industry magnates, Andrew Carnegie, George Westinghouse and Henry Clay Frick, built their factories and their fortunes here.

The two travelers arrived in Pittsburgh in late November, 1831. They had made their way through swirling winds and heavy snow to reach the town. Beaumont wrote that their journey from Philadelphia was cloaked in "a perpetual tornado of snow." It

There are 720 bridges within Pittsburgh's city limits.

Pittsburgh, 1830

Hog Wild

In the mid-1800s, the streets of Pittsburgh were strewn with mud. Wild dogs and pigs ran unchecked in the muck-covered streets. In the 1850s, reports of savage pigs attacking children grew so numerous that authorities established a pig pound. A one-dollar reward was paid for each pig caught. Even as late as the 1860s, records show that 39 pigs were impounded in one day.

was the Frenchmen's first taste of the harsh winter that continued to plague them for their tour of the South. The Frenchmen stayed in Pittsburgh "but an instant," yet were able to manage a tour of the Western Penitentiary of Pennsylvania, then located in the city. The prison failed to impress Tocqueville and Beaumont. They found 64 idle inmates in unkempt cells. Unlike most of the other American prisons they had visited, where silence was strictly enforced, inmates talked to one another unchecked.

Tocqueville attributed the penitentiary's air of neglect to the townspeople's lack of interest in prison reform. "In a government where strength and continuity are nowhere to be found, those things only are well done that excite the interest of the public and that yield glory and profit on that account to the individuals who take a hand in them," the Frenchmen would later write in their prison report.

What to See

Senator John Heinz Pittsburgh Regional History Center

This new museum details the story of Pittsburgh's past, including stories about the city's involvement with the escape route for slaves known as the underground railroad. Photographs and artifacts focus on city history and the lives of its illustrious residents.
1212 Smallman Street.
Tel: (412) 454-6000.

Frick Art & Historical Center

Henry Clay Frick's six-acre estate features the industry giant's restored house, an art museum and a historic carriage museum. The center also has a café which serves high tea and is listed as one of the city's best restaurants.
7227 Reynolds Street.
Tel: (412) 371-0600.

The Monongahela and Duquesne Inclines

Pittsburgh's inclines, rail cars built to travel steep hills, were constructed in the late 1800s, during the height of the industrial age, to carry people and freight up the city's hills. The Monongahela opened in 1870 and carried people from the top of Coal Hill (today Mt. Washington) to jobs below in the factories that lined the river. The Duquesne Incline

122 View from Mt. Washington

Pittsburgh skyline

was opened in 1877. Both inclines still operate today. At the top of the Duquesne Incline an observation deck offers dramatic views of Pittsburgh's three rivers. Both located on Grandview Avenue. Monongahela Incline. Tel: (412) 488-3085. Duquesne Incline Tel: (412) 381-1665.

Pennsylvania Trolley Museum

Visitors can take a ride on a restored trolley car and learn about the age of the trolley. Exhibits feature more than 100 photos documenting the life of the men and women who worked for America's trolley companies. One Museum Road, Washington. Tel: (412) 228-9256.

Fort Pitt Museum

Built by the British in 1758, Fort Pitt is located on the triangular jut of land where the Allegheny and Monongahela Rivers meet to form the Ohio River. The museum documents the 18th-century battle between the French and British to control the American frontier. Every Sunday, from mid-June through Labor Day, volunteers dress in full British regalia to recreate the sights and sounds of the British army who built and manned the fort. 101 Commonwealth Place in Point State Park. Tel: (412) 281-9284.

Pittsburgh *Today*

Pittsburgh has made one of the great urban comebacks of this century. Once known world over for its industry and its polluted environment, city officials began a process of renewal a few years after World War II; by 1985, Pittsburgh ranked in the top five most livable cities in the *Places Rated Almanac*. The city is also known for its corporate headquarters. Westinghouse, H.J. Heinz and PPG Industries make their home here. More than 300,000 people live in Pittsburgh.

Inns and Outs

How to get there:
From the east, follow I-76 (Pennsylvania Turnpike) west to Pittsburgh which takes you directly into the city. For a more scenic route, try I-68 west along the Maryland border, until you reach Morgantown where you take I-79 north. From the south, follow I-79 north to Pittsburgh.

T he Pittsburgh Pirates, the city's first professional baseball team, went through a couple of names before finding their present one. First, they were the Alleghenies and later spent a season as the Innocents. In 1891, Manager Ed Hanlon signed a new infielder from another team; people called the signing an "act of piracy" and the team's new name was born.

Where to stay:
For lodging information contact the Greater Pittsburgh Chamber of Commerce. 3 Gateway Center, 14th Floor, Pittsburgh, PA 15222. Tel: (412) 392-4500. Also try the Pittsburgh Convention and Visitors Bureau.
4 Gateway Center, Suite 1800, Pittsburgh, PA 15222. Tel: (800) 359-0758.

Other Attractions

Carnegie Science Center
Situated in a four-story, domed theater, the Science Center displays distant galaxies in its planetarium and offers more than 250 exhibits, including a miniature railroad and a WWII submarine.
One Allegheny Avenue. Tel: (412) 237-3400.

The Andy Warhol Museum
This museum provides an in-depth look at the pop artist's life and work. The collection includes drawings, paintings, sculpture, film, video tapes and more. The *Weekend Factory* is an ongoing exhibit that allows visitors to try Warhol's techniques on canvas and silk screen.
117 Sandusky Street. Tel: (412) 237-8300.

Carnegie Museums of Art and Natural History
Paintings, sculptures and decorative arts from ancient Greece to modern day are housed here. The Natural History Museum offers exhibits including displays on dinosaurs, Egyptian mummies and other artifacts from ancient Egypt. 4400 Forbes Avenue. Tel: (412) 622-3131.

The Pittsburgh Zoo
More than 4,000 animals live at this renowned zoo. Visitors will discover an Asian forest, an AquaZoo complete with a living coral reef, penguins and a shark tank.
One Hill Road. Tel: (412) 665-3640.

The *Gateway Party Liner*

"This river flows for quite a while between enclosing mountains. These mountains, a chain of the Alleghenies, offer a prodigious variety of sites, each more picturesque than the last. After a day on the water we arrived within a league of a small town named Wheeling."

—Gustave de Beaumont

Wheeling
West Virginia

Wheeling is perched high in the Allegheny Mountains overlooking the Ohio River. A walk through Old Town Wheeling reveals elegant Victorian mansions lining the riverbanks. They were once the homes of wealthy merchants who made their fortunes by capitalizing on the frenzied commercial trade along the river.

Today the industrial fever that dominated the town in the 1800s has quieted, and Wheeling is laying the groundwork for a new economy based on historic preservation, entertainment and tourism.

Tocqueville and Beaumont almost didn't make it to Wheeling. Toward midnight on November 26, while traveling down the Ohio River aboard the *Fourth of July,* their steamship hit a rock on the Burlington Bar reef; water rushed into the ship.

"The Ohio charged with blocks of ice. Its banks covered with snow...our boat has stove itself in; it is going down before one's eyes. olemn moment: two hundred passengers aboard, and only two skiffs each able to hold ten to a dozen persons.

The water rises, rises; it already fills the cabins," is how Beaumont later described the crash.

Icy deaths were averted: as the boat sank it caught on a rock and managed to remain somewhat afloat. The passengers were rescued and brought ashore; Tocqueville and Beaumont spent the night in a cold hut.

The next day, another steamship picked them up and carried them to Wheeling. The two travelers, anxious to reach the Mississippi River and New Orleans, did not spend a long time in town.

> West Virginia's motto is *Montani Semper Liberi* or "Mountaineers Are Always Free."

Beaumont's sketch of the Burlington Bar Reef

The 35th State

When Tocqueville and Beaumont visited Wheeling in 1831, the state of West Virginia did not exist. Instead, Wheeling was part of Virginia which stretched clear across the Allegheny Mountains. During the years leading up to the Civil War, differences arose between the eastern and western areas of the state, primarily concerning slavery. Slave-holders in the eastern part of the state had more representation in the state legislature than the mostly slave-free western part of the state. Tensions came to a head when the Virginia government in Richmond seceded from the Union in April 1861. Meetings were held in Wheeling's Independence Hall, and western delegates declared the Richmond government void; a "restored government of Virginia" was formed. On June 20, 1863, Abraham Lincoln, by executive order, decreed West Virginia the 35th state in the union.

What to See

Historic Victorian Wheeling

The Victorian Wheeling Landmark Foundation offers tours of Wheeling's Victorian houses. PO Box 667, Wheeling, WV 26003. Tel: (304) 233-1600.

Wheeling's Suspension Bridge, built in 1849, was the first bridge to span the Ohio River and was the world's longest bridge at the time.

West Virginia Independence Hall

Once the old Custom House, Independence Hall is considered the birthplace of West Virginia. During the Civil War, great debates over the separation of West Virginia and Virginia were waged here. Costumed interpreters, period rooms and exhibits bring the story to life. 1528 Market Street. Tel: (304) 238-1300.

Point Overlook Museum

Located 565 feet above the Ohio River, this museum gives visitors a picture of what Wheeling looked like a century ago as well as a panoramic view of the city today. The museum features rare 19th- and 20th-century photos of the city. 989 Grandview Street. Tel: (304) 232-3010.

Centre Market

Shops, restaurants and boutiques are all housed in this renovated 19th-century market house. 22nd and Market Streets. Tel: (304) 234-3878.

Wheeling Today

People come from miles around to see Wheeling's festival of lights, held each November through January in Oglebay Park. The show includes more than 300 acres of lighted displays and landscapes and is the largest light show in the nation. The city's industry includes metal, paper products and plastics. Today more than 34,000 people live in Wheeling.

126   Beaumont's sketch of Wheeling

Wheeling's Oglebay Park

Inns *and* Outs

How to get there:
Follow the Pennsylvania Turnpike west to exit 8. Pick up Route 70 west which leads to Wheeling.

Where to stay:
For lodging information, contact the Wheeling Convention and Visitors Bureau.
1310 Market Street,
Suite 1000,
Wheeling, WV 26003.
Tel: (800) 828-3097 or
(304) 233-7709.
www.wheelingcvb.com

Other Attractions

Wheeling Artisan Center
Visitors can get a feel for Wheeling history in this restored industrial building. The second floor emporium is a mix of crafts, shopping and history with artisans demonstrating their crafts and exhibits along the walls. **Wymer's General Store Museum** is a recreated 1880s general store complete with antiques and other memorabilia.
1400 Main Street.
Tel: (304) 232-1810

Oglebay Park
Wheeling operates a 1,650-acre resort famous for its winter festival of lights. The resort offers tennis courts, golf courses, fishing, swimming, boating and a zoo. Visitors can also wander the red brick paths through Waddington Gardens which recreate many turn-of-the-century gardens. The Oglebay museums include the **Mansion Museum,** a fine columned house built in 1846 and owned by Earl Oglebay. At his death, Oglebay left his house and estate to the town. Inside the Carriage House, the **Glass Museum** contains the largest collection of Wheeling glass in the world. Both museums are operated through the Museums of Oglebay Institute. On Route 88N.
Tel: (304) 242-4200.

Jamboree USA/ Capitol Music Hall
The Capitol Music Hall features live country music, Las Vegas-style shows and the Wheeling Symphony Orchestra. "Jamboree USA" is broadcast live from here to more than 18 states and eight Canadian provinces.
1015 Main Street.
Tel: (800) 624-5456.

Look for the C-SPAN plaque, marking Tocqueville's visit, on the exterior viewing deck of the Point Overlook Museum.

127

> *"Great buildings, thatched cottages, streets encumbered with debris, houses under construction, no names on the streets, no numbers on the houses, no outward luxury, but the image of industry and labour obvious at every step."*
>
> —Alexis de Tocqueville

Cincinnati
Ohio

In warm weather, crowds gather in Cincinnati's Fountain Square for lunch time concerts. Tall glass office buildings, including the Carew Tower, the city's highest structure, surround the square. In the center of the plaza, the Tyler Davidson Fountain, erected in 1871 as an ode to the power of water, depicts a woman with water flowing from her fingertips.

And it is to water—specifically the mighty Ohio River—that Cincinnati owes much

Located at the foot of Broadway, the Public Landing was once the site of the city's first log cabin and also the center of Cincinnati's river trade.

of its development. In the late 1700s, the river, which forms the Kentucky/Ohio border, carried the city's first settlers. During the 19th century, the river gained importance as one of America's primary routes to the West. Cincinnati took advantage of its location along the Ohio River to become a major supplier of goods and produce.

When Tocqueville and Beaumont arrived by steamboat on the first of December 1831, the town was a busy commercial center. The city's rapid growth amazed the two men. It was the most curious town Beaumont

Cincinnati Landing, 1848

Cincinnati, Ohio

Porkopolis

In the 1840s, Cincinnati slaughtered an average of 375,000 pigs a year. The city became one of the pork-packing capitals of America and earned the nickname "Porkopolis." During a stay in Cincinnati in 1842, Charles Dickens wrote, " [Cincinnati] is in fact what its nickname, 'Porkopolis' implies—the Empire City of Pigs, as well as of the West; but it is fortunate that they condescendingly allow human beings to share that truly magnificent location with them."

had ever seen. "I don't believe there exists anywhere on earth, a town which has had a growth so prodigious. Thirty years ago the banks of the Ohio were a wilderness. Now there are 30,000 inhabitants in Cincinnati."

The French nobles used letters of introduction to meet some of Cincinnati's most prominent citizens. One man, Timothy Walker, a young Harvard graduate, talked to Tocqueville about slavery. Tocqueville had looked across the river toward Covington, Kentucky and was puzzled by the strangely tranquil and pastoral scene.

Tocqueville asked Walker to explain. Walker told him, "... slavery reigns in Kentucky and not in Ohio. There work is dishonourable, here held in esteem. There there is laziness, here activity without limit."

It was a contrast that Tocqueville did not forget. In *Democracy in America* he wrote, "Upon the left bank of the Ohio labor is confounded with the idea of slavery, while upon the right bank it is identified with that of prosperity and improvement..."

What to See

Taft Museum

Housed in a restored Federal-style mansion, the Taft Museum started with the collection of Anna Sinton and Charles Phelps Taft. Today the museum contains hundreds of pieces, including portraits by Rembrandt and Hals as well as Chinese porcelains and Italian-carved crystals. Grounds include a formal garden. 316 Pike Street. Tel: (513) 241-0343.

Harriet Beecher Stowe House

When Abraham Lincoln met Harriet Beecher Stowe, author of *Uncle Tom's Cabin,* he reportedly said, "So you are the little lady who wrote the book that made this great war." Stowe moved to Cincinnati in 1832 and lived in this simple two-story gabled house. The house is open for tours and features displays on the Beecher family and the abolitionist movement. 2950 Gilbert Avenue. Tel: (513) 632-5120.

The city is famous for its chili. Spiced with cinnamon, Cincinnati chili is usually served over spaghetti and smothered in cheese.

129

William Howard Taft Home

The century-old boyhood home of William Howard Taft, the 27th President and 10th Chief Justice of the Supreme Court, contains period furnishings and exhibits on Taft's life.
2038 Auburn Avenue.
Tel: (513) 684-3262.

Cincinnati Museum Center

Two museums and a huge theater are housed in Union Terminal, a renovated art deco train station. **The Cincinnati History Museum** houses exhibits on the city's historic development from a frontier town to a modern urban center. Displays include an 1850s reconstruction of Public Landing where the city's first settlers came ashore, and a World War II retrospective, featuring a gas station and a streetcar. In the **Cincinnati Museum of Natural History and Science,** visitors can explore a simulation of an underground waterfall and a limestone cavern. The **OMNIMAX theater,** which features a five-story-high, 72-foot-wide screen, shows educational and entertainment films and surrounds viewers with super-sized images and quality sound. Union Terminal, 1301 Western Avenue.
Tel: (800) 733-2077.

Sharon Woods Village

This 30-acre village revisits life in Ohio before the 1880s. Nine reconstructed buildings are furnished with period articles including a medical office, an 1800s barn and a log cabin. Located within Sharon Woods Park, one mile south of I-275, exit 46 on US 42.
Open April through October.
Tel: (513) 563-9484.

Cincinnati
Today

Cincinnati's recently renovated downtown and riverfront area is a popular recreational spot. Major hotels, restaurants and office buildings are all connected by an enclosed skywalk. The city has several parks offering scenic views of the Ohio River Valley. Eden Park on Gilbert Avenue between Elsinore and Morris overlooks the river and the rolling Kentucky Hills.
Directly southwest of the

130 Tyler Davidson Fountain

Cincinnati from the Ohio River

park is the Mt. Adams area. Sometimes called the Monmartre of Cincinnati, its narrow streets, small restaurants and boutiques give it a European flavor. Cincinnati has a population of more than 350,000 and is home to the University of Cincinnati and Xavier University.

Inns *and* Outs

How to get there:
From the north or south take I-75 or I-71. Both roads lead into downtown Cincinnati. From the east or west, take US 50 or US 52. US 52 offers a view of the Ohio River east of Cincinnati.

Where to stay:
For lodging information contact the Greater Cincinnati Convention & Visitors Bureau. 300 West 6th Street, Cincinnati, OH 45202. Tel: (513) 621-2142. Information is also available from the Greater Cincinnati

Chamber of Commerce. 300 Carew Tower, 441 Vine Street, Cincinnati, OH 45202. Tel: (513) 579-3100.

Other Attractions

Cincinnati Art Museum
This extensive collection stretches across 5,000 years and includes art from ancient Egypt, Greece and Rome. Also on display are furniture, glass, silver, costumes, folk art and African art. 953 Eden Park Drive. Tel: (513) 721-5204.

Cincinnati Zoo and Botanical Garden
A Komodo dragon, white Bengal tigers and rare Sumatran rhinos live at the Cincinnati Zoo. With more than 700 species of live animals, the 70-acre zoo also includes a rain forest exhibit and the nation's first and largest insectarium. 3400 Vine Street. Tel: (513) 281-4701.

131

> *"We passed through the whole breadth of Kentucky...The country is covered with hills and shallow valleys through which a multitude of little streams flow; it is a land of natural, but uniform, beauty."*

> —Alexis de Tocqueville

Lousiville & Westport
Kentucky

On the first Saturday in May, Louisville plays host to the Kentucky Derby where, for two short minutes, the fastest horses in the world gallop past the Edwardian twin spires at Churchill Downs and into horse racing history. The first Kentucky Derby was held in 1875, just forty years after Tocqueville and Beaumont visited.

The two voyagers stopped briefly in both Ohio River ports. They arrived in Louisville on December 6, 1831 at nine o'clock at night, after having walked 25 miles through snow-covered

Look for the C-SPAN plaque commemorating Tocqueville's visit to Louisville on the Jefferson County Courthouse at 527 West Jefferson Street.

forests from Westport. Their days had been plagued with mishaps. Their first steamship ran aground. And, their second steamship was forced to dock at Westport when the Ohio River froze. For the two men, Louisville literally was a safe harbor in the storm.

Travel difficulties did not deter Tocqueville's quest to understand America. While waiting for the ice to break, he interviewed B.R. McIlvaine, a wealthy merchant, about Kentucky's economics.

McIlvaine's business was booming, but the merchant felt that slavery was hampering Kentucky's growth. "...slavery prevents the emigrants coming to us. They deprive us of the

Downtown Louisville, 1830

132

Run for the Roses

Derby lore has it that in 1883 all the ladies attending a race party were given roses by their host, New York socialite and gamester E. Berry Wall. Colonel M. Lewis Clark, track president, was so taken by the enthusiastic response of the ladies that he adopted the rose as the Derby's official flower. More than fifty years later, Bill Corum, a New York sports columnist, coined the phrase "Run for the Roses." Today the Derby-winning horse is adorned with a blanket of 500 dark-red American Beauty roses.

energy and enterprising spirit which characterizes the states where there are no slaves," the merchant told Tocqueville.

Tocqueville and Beaumont did not stay long in Louisville. Their plans to travel by steamboat down the Ohio to the Mississippi and on to New Orleans were thwarted when they learned that the whole length of the Ohio River was frozen.

"There was a third alternative to be taken, however. On the banks of the Mississip[p]i, in the State of Tennessee, we were told there was a small town, called Memphis, where all the steamboats going up or coming down the river stop to take on wood. If we could reach this place we would be sure to resume our navigation, as the Mississip[p]i never freezes," wrote Beaumont.

The Frenchmen opted to try the Mississippi and, braving the bitter cold, set out in an open carriage toward Memphis.

What to See

The Kentucky Derby Museum

Visitors can tour Churchill Downs and visit the museum's resident thoroughbred and miniature horses. The museum features exhibits on thoroughbred breeding, betting and racing. Multi-image shows and hands-on displays are part of the fun. 704 Central Avenue, Louisville. Tel: (502) 637-7097.

Locust Grove Historic Home

One of Kentucky's oldest plantation houses, Locust Grove was built in 1790 and was once the home of Louisville's founder, General George Rogers Clark. Situated on 55 acres, the Georgian mansion also includes restored outbuildings and gardens. American Presidents James Monroe, Andrew Jackson and Zachary Taylor all slept here. 561 Blankenbaker Lane, Louisville. Tel: (502) 897-9845.

Farmington Historic Home

This Federal-style house was built from Thomas Jefferson's blueprints. Completed in 1810, the house's furnishings include period antiques. Look for Jefferson's signature octagonal rooms. On the grounds are a blacksmith shop, a stone barn and a 19th-century garden. Guided tours are available. 3033 Bardstown Road, Louisville. Tel: (502) 452-9920.

The Mint Julep, a drink made from bourbon, sugar water and mint, was adopted in 1939 as the official drink of the Kentucky Derby.

Louisville Slugger Museum

Visitors can't miss the giant wooden bat which leans against the Louisville Slugger Museum. The museum chronicles the history of Hillerich & Bradsby Company which has been making baseball bats for more than a century.

The museum includes a full size dugout, rare baseball memorabilia and a replica of a white ash forest (the wood from which many of the bats are made). An interactive display allows visitors to "step up to the plate" and face a 90-mph fastball with a Louisville Slugger in their hands. Next door, a giant baseball is seemingly lodged in the window of the factory where the bats are fashioned. 800 West Main Street, Louisville. Tel: (502) 588-7228.

Louisville's Falls Fountain in the Ohio River is the tallest computerized floating fountain in the world. It uses colored lights and more than 40 jets to pump water 400 feet into the air.

Belle of Louisville

The oldest Mississippi-style stern wheeler still in use, the *Belle of Louisville* gives visitors a sense of the steamboat travel of yesteryear. The ornate *Belle* takes visitors for two-hour afternoon trips along the Ohio River. It is usually moored at the wharf at 4th Street and River Road, Louisville. Tel: (502) 574-2355.

Louisville & Westport *Today*

With a population of 270,000, Louisville is Kentucky's largest city. The city has earned a reputation as a center for the arts and is home to the Louisville Orchestra, the Kentucky Opera and the Louisville Ballet. A public subscription, *Fund for the Arts,* subsidizes the city's award-winning Actors Theater.

The city's Main Street, with its renovated buildings, looks much the way it did in the late 18th century. Butchertown, a 19th-century German community, retains traces of its old flavor. Louisville is a top producer of bourbon, cigarettes and paint; it is also headquarters for corporations such as United

The Delta Queen Steamboat

The Louisville skyline

Parcel Service, Humana and the KFC Corporation.

Westport now has a population of approximately 500 people and two businesses.

One is the River Town General Store, where many residents gather to talk about the day's events.

Inns *and* Outs

How to get there:
From Cincinnati take I-75 south to I-71 to Louisville. From Nashville take I-65 north into the city. From the east or west, take I-64 to Louisville.

To reach Westport from Louisville take I-71 north to US Highway 42. Take State Highway 524 to Westport.

Where to stay:
For lodging information contact the Louisville Convention & Visitors Bureau.
400 South First Street, Louisville, KY 40202.
Tel: (502) 584-2121 or (800) 626-5646.

Other Attractions

J.B. Speed Art Museum
The oldest and largest museum in the state includes more than 5,000 pieces of art, spanning 6,000 years. The museum houses galleries with various concentrations, including African, Native-American, and Kentucky/American art. The collection also includes works by Rembrandt, Rubens and Monet.
2035 South 3rd Street, Louisville. Tel: (502) 634-2700.

Louisville Science Center
Kid friendly, this museum features interactive displays which allow visitors to dock a space freighter, design a bicycle, or build a bridge. Visitors can explore everything from the workings of the human hand to the artifacts from an ancient Egyptian tomb.
727 West Main Street, Louisville.
Tel: (502) 561-6100.

Near the Westport Community Commons, on the corner of Highway 524 and 4th Street, a C-SPAN plaque has been placed as a reminder of Tocqueville's historic visit.

135

Nashville
Tennessee

Situated along the banks of the Cumberland River, the capital city of Tennessee is often called "Music City USA." Sounds of country music broadcast live each Friday and Saturday night from the Grand Old Opry stage. The city has lately enjoyed both a high job growth rate and one of the lowest costs of living in the nation.

When Tocqueville and Beaumont reached Nashville on December 10, 1831, it was a picturesque town confined to a single bluff on the bank of the Cumberland River. About 6,000 people lived in the city which boasted stately red brick houses, a court house, two banks, a public library and an academy for women.

In 1831, Nashville was one of most prominent towns in the state. Growing rapidly, it had gained considerable importance as President Andrew Jackson's home town and became the permanent capital of Tennessee in 1843.

Tocqueville did not stay long in Nashville and mentioned very little about the town in his journal. Instead he was intrigued with the log cabin settlers whom he met in the wilds of Tennessee. "After passing over a fence of roughly shaped wood ... one reaches a cabin through whose walls a fire can be seen crackling

Tocqueville and Beaumont most likely stayed at the Nashville Inn which was the town's finest hostelry in the 1830s. It was destroyed by fire in 1856 and stood at the spot where the Metro Courthouse now stands.

View of Nashville's Public Square, circa 1830

on the hearth... one enters a sort of savage hut which seems the refuge of every misery; there one finds a poor family living with the leisure of the rich," he wrote.

Tocqueville was struck by the number of newspapers and letters that circulated in the wilderness and was impressed with how well-informed the people were.

In a letter home he wrote, "Nothing in Kentucky or Tennessee gives the impression of such a finished society... But yet they are by no means still rustic folk; there is none of that simplicity bred of ignorance and prejudices... which distinguish agricultural peoples in the least accessible places. These men nonetheless belong to one of the most civilised and rational peoples in the world."

What to See

Tennessee State Museum

Davy Crockett's rifle, Sam Houston's guitar and Andrew Jackson's inaugural top hat are all housed in the Tennessee State Museum. The museum traces Tennessee history from prehistoric times to the early 1900s and contains the largest collection of Civil War artifacts from western battles in the country.
505 Deaderick Street.
Tel: (615) 741-2692.

The Hermitage

The Hermitage

This Greek-Revival plantation was the home of President Andrew Jackson and his beloved wife Rachel. It was built in 1819 and remodeled after a fire in 1834. The mansion is furnished with original pieces and nearly all of Jackson's personal effects. The 650-acre historic treasure includes the Jackson family graveyard and two log cabins where Jackson lived from 1804-1821. 4580 Rachel's Lane, Hermitage.
Tel: (615) 889-2941.

Look for the C-SPAN plaque in the Freedom Forum's First Amendment Center. Located on the campus of Vanderbilt University, the center's goal is to improve the public's understanding and appreciation for First Amendment rights. 1207 18th Avenue South.

Originally called the Barn Dance, the Grand Ole Opry got its name one evening after following a broadcast of the New York Opera. Announcer George D. Hay introduced the show with, "Folks, for the past hour we've been listening to music taken largely from the Grand Opera. Well y'all just sit right back, because from now on, you're gonna hear the Grand Ole Opry."

Opryland USA

One of Nashville's most famous landmarks, this entertainment complex includes the **Grand Ole Opry** performance house. From its stage, 70 years of country music have been broadcast on the world's longest running radio show. 2804 Opryland Drive. The **Grand Ole Opry Museum** pays tribute to country music stars, including legends such as Patsy Cline, Jim Reeves, Bill Monroe and other country music pioneers. 2802 Opryland Drive.

General Jackson, a 300-foot deck paddle-wheel showboat, offers cruises on the Cumberland River. One phone number answers all questions about tickets and exhibit information. Tel: (615) 889-6611.

Travellers Rest Historic House Museum

The 1799 restored Federal-style house of Judge John Overton includes formal gardens, a kitchen and a smokehouse. Overton was the law partner, campaign manager and a lifelong friend of Andrew Jackson. The house contains furnishings from the 1800s and Overton family records and letters. 636 Farrell Parkway. Tel: (615) 832-8197.

Fort Nashborough

The fort, a replica of the original built in 1779, gives visitors a glimpse of Nashville's frontier life. 170 1st Avenue North, in Riverfront Park. Tel: (615) 862-8424.

Belle Meade Plantation

Belle Meade is known as the "Queen of the Tennessee Plantations." The Greek-Revival mansion features 14-foot ceilings and a spectacular curving staircase. The plantation was once the setting of lavish parties. It was

The Grand Ole Opry

The Parthenon's Athena and Elgin Marbles

also the premier thoroughbred breeding farm in the country. In 1881, *Iroquois* was the first American horse to win the English Derby. *Secretariat,* the famous Kentucky Derby winner, was also bred here. Located on the grounds is an 18th-century carriage collection.
5025 Harding Road.
Tel: (615) 356-0501 or
(800) 270-3991.

Parthenon
This replica of the Parthenon was built for the Tennessee Centennial in 1897. The citizens of Nashville liked it so much they decided to make it permanent. Today it houses 19th- and 20th-century art as well as changing exhibits. The Parthenon is home to a 42-foot sculpture of the goddess Athena. It is the largest indoor statue in the western world.
West End Avenue,
in Centennial Park.
Tel: (615) 862-8431.

Carter House
Located 15 miles outside of Nashville, this cotton farm was built in 1830. During the Civil War, the Battle of Franklin raged around it. Today visitors can tour the farm house which is still riddled with more than 1,000 bullet holes from the battle. Exhibits focus on Tennessee life in the 1830s.
1140 Columbia Avenue.
Tel: (615) 791-1861.

Carnton Plantation
Built in 1826 by former Nashville mayor Randal McGavock, this antebellum mansion with its gracious front porch and white columns was used as a field hospital during the Civil War Battle of Franklin. Hundreds of wounded soldiers were carted to the house. The back porch held the bodies of Generals Cleburne, Granbury, Strahl and Adams. The McGavock Confederate Cemetery with 1,500 graves is located on the plantation grounds.
1345 Carnton Lane, Franklin.
Tel: (615) 794-0903.

Museum of Tobacco Art and History
This interesting little museum reflects the role tobacco has played in the social and economic development of the United States. Early advertisements, pipes from every part of the world and intricately carved snuff boxes are on display. 800 Harrison Street.
Tel: (615) 271-2349.

Nashville from the shores of the Cumberland River

Nashville *Today*

Along with music—religion, arts and education are a Nashville tradition. There are 16 colleges and universities located here as well as religious publishing firms and more than 700 churches. This has helped the city earn the nickname "Athens of the South." Tourism is one of the leading industries with Opryland being one of the city's most popular attractions. More than 500,000 people live in Nashville.

Inns and Outs

How to get there:
From the north/south, take I-65 into Nashville. From the east/west, take I-40.

Where to stay:
For lodging and tourist information contact the Nashville Convention and Visitors Bureau. 161 Fourth Avenue North, Nashville, TN 37219. Tel: (615) 259-4730. www.musiccityusa.citysearch.com Also try the Nashville Visitors Information Center. 501 Broadway, Nashville, TN 37203. Tel: (615) 259-4747.

Other Attractions

Country Music Hall of Fame and Museum
This museum gives visitors a behind-the-scenes look at the world of country music. Films and exhibits honor musicians and others who have contributed to country music. Costumes and artifacts, including Elvis Presley's "solid gold" Cadillac and gold piano, are on display. 4 Music Square East. Tel: (615) 256-1639 or (800) 816-7652.

Nashville Toy Museum
Visitors can explore the history of toys through the museum's internationally known collection of antique toys including model trains, antique dolls, early teddy bears and toy soldiers. 2613 McGavock Pike. Tel: (615) 883-8870.

Cheekwood: Nashville's Home of Art and Gardens
This Georgian-style mansion was once the home of the Cheek family who made their fortune with Maxwell House Coffee. Today it is an art museum containing 19th- and 20th-century American paintings situated on 55 acres of gardens, woodlands and greenhouses. Flower and gardening displays are housed in Botanic Hall. The Pineapple Room Restaurant serves plenty of Southern cooking. 1200 Forrest Park Drive. Tel: (615) 356-8000.

140

Memphis
Tennessee

On Memphis' Beale Street, once the home of gin mills, dice parlors and pool halls, the blues were born. The legendary blues guitarist, B.B. King, made his home here and was originally known as the "Beale Street Blues Boy."

As a young boy in Memphis, Elvis Presley absorbed the rhythms and gospel stylings that poured out of the city's night clubs and churches. Here, Presley built his mansion, Graceland, one of the most visited houses in the U.S.

In 1831, however, when Tocqueville and Beaumont arrived, Memphis was a small Mississippi River town. According to Beaumont, there was little to see and few diversions. The two men arrived on December 17, after an arduous overland journey. Due in part to the bitter cold of 1831, Tocqueville fell ill on the route between Nashville and Memphis.

Beaumont later described the journey: "... the cold still more rigorous; we cross the Tennessee, carrying down great cakes of ice, in a ferry. Tocqueville benumbed by cold; he experiences a chill. He has lost his appetite; his head affected; impossible to go any further, we must stop...Where? How? No inn on the road. Extreme anguish...Here finally is a house [called]: Sandy-Bridge." After four days, with Beaumont nursing him, Tocqueville regained his strength and the two men were able to reach Memphis.

During the week, while waiting for a steamship to break through the ice and carry them down the Mississippi, they went bird hunting in the Tennessee forests. "But for the worry, however, these days passed pleasantly enough. We were staying with some nice people who did their best to be agreeable to us.

While working at PeeWee's Saloon on Beale Street in 1912, W.C. Handy wrote "Memphis Blues" and introduced America to a new form of music. For this, he earned the title, "Father of the Blues."

B.B. King's Blues Club and Restaurant

141

The King of Rock and Roll

Elvis Presley acquired his first guitar at age 11. He would have preferred a bicycle, but his parents were unable to afford one and talked him into accepting a guitar. It was a historic decision. Presley would go on to sell more than one billion recordings worldwide, more than any other artist or group in history.

Aboard the steamship heading from Memphis to New Orleans, Tocqueville met Sam Houston, the former Governor of Tennessee who would lead the Texas army to a brilliant victory over Santa Anna in the Battle of San Jacinto. Houston later helped bring Texas into the Union. Tocqueville described him as: "...everything in [Houston's] person indicates physical and moral energy."

Twenty paces from our house began the most admirable forest, the most sublime and picturesque place in the world, even in the snow."

Later as Tocqueville and Beaumont stood on the river bank waiting to board a steamboat to leave Memphis, they witnessed, "a large troup of Indians, old men, women, children, belongings, all led by a European."

As a result of the Indian Removal Act of 1830, which had been signed into law by President Andrew Jackson, Native Americans east of the Mississippi River, including elderly, frail women and sick children, were being forced to leave their ancestral lands. Tocqueville and Beaumont watched disconsolately as men,

women and children boarded the ship to journey from their ancestral homes to new lands in Oklahoma. For Tocqueville there was in the whole scene, "an air of ruin and destruction, something which betrayed a final and irrevocable adieu; one couldn't watch without feeling one's heart wrung."

What to See

Graceland

A visit to Memphis would not be complete without a tour of the King's house. Visitors can see his trophy room, containing Elvis' gold records, awards, costumes and photographs. A short film unfolds in the fifties-style drive-in theater.

Meditation Garden is the site of Elvis' grave. The Elvis Presley Automobile Museum is also located in Graceland and includes a collection of the King's cars, including a green and a pink Cadillac.
3717 Elvis Presley Boulevard.
Tel: (800) 238-2000.

Center for Southern Folklore

The center has books, films and tours to give visitors a sense of the South including a documentary on blues legend W.C. Handy and tours of local farming communities.
209 Beale Street.
Tel: (901) 525-3655.

Graceland

Memphis, Tennessee

Pyramid Arena

Pyramid Arena

Memphis, named for the great Egyptian city on the Nile, is also home to a 32-story pyramid overlooking the Mississippi River. The Pyramid contains a music, sports and entertainment complex. One Auction Avenue in the downtown Pinch Historic District on the Wolf River. Tel: (901) 521-9675.

National Civil Rights Museum

The Lorraine Motel where Dr. Martin Luther King was assassinated on April 4, 1968 is now a museum devoted to documenting the American civil rights struggle. Exhibits explore the Montgomery, Alabama Bus Boycott, student sit-ins and the march from Selma to Montgomery, Alabama. Racial tensions have been a critical element of Memphis since riots broke out in 1866; these early riots were a precursor to eruptions that would occur a century later. 450 Mulberry Street. Tel: (901) 521-9699.

Mud Island

Situated on an island in the river is a park dedicated to the Mississippi River. Visitors can walk the five-block-long scaled model of the great river, which stretches from Cairo, IL to the Gulf of Mexico. The Mississippi River Museum features a life-size reproduction of an 1870s steamboat and exhibits tracing the history, art and lore of the river. Mud Island is also home to the *Memphis Belle,* a B-17 bomber that survived 25 missions over Nazi targets during World War II. A monorail located at the intersection of Front Street and Poplar Avenue brings tourists to the island. Tel: (800) 507-6507.

Memphis Pink Palace Mansion, Museum, Planetarium and Theater

This huge pink marble mansion was designed to be the home of Clarence Saunders, founder of the Piggly Wiggly grocery store chain. Today the museum allows visitors to explore the South through exhibits and audio-visual presentations. The museum traces the history of Memphis from the time of Spanish explorers to today. 3050 Central Avenue. Tel: (901) 320-6320.

Pink Palace Museum

Memphis nightscape

The Peabody Hotel

Memphis' premier hotel, the Peabody, was built in 1869 and was the place to be seen for Southern society. William McKinley, Robert E. Lee and William Faulkner all stayed here. The hotel is famous for its ducks which march from their duck penthouse on the roof to a fountain in the lobby promptly at 11o'clock each day. 149 Union Avenue. Tel: (800) PEABODY (732-2639).

Memphis
Today

Memphis, with a population of more than 600,000, is the largest city in Tennessee and the cotton capital of the U.S. The city has a distinct spirit and is famous for its music and Memphis barbecue. Located on the Mississippi River and one of the primary cities in the mid-south, Memphis is a distribution hub for the rest of the country. Federal Express, Dunavant Enterprises, one of the world's largest cotton merchandising companies, and International Paper have built their headquarters here.

Look for the C-SPAN plaque in Tom Lee Park on Riverside Drive, along the banks of the Mississippi River.

Inns and Outs

How to get there:

From east or west, take I-40 to I-240. Or, from the east, take I-72 west through Germantown. From north or south, take I-55 to I-240.

Where to stay:

For lodging information, contact the Memphis Convention & Visitors Bureau. 119 North Riverside Drive (walk-in); 47 Union Avenue, Memphis, TN 38103 (mailing address). Tel: (901) 543-5333. The Memphis Area Chamber of Commerce is also a resource. 22 North Front Street, Suite 200, Memphis, TN 38103. Tel: (901) 575-3500.

Other Attractions

Memphis Botanic Gardens

Visitors will discover a dogwood trail along with Japanese, cactus, sculpture and herb gardens at the Botanic Gardens. 750 Cherry Road in Audubon Park. Tel: (901) 685-1566.

Memphis Brooks Museum of Art

This museum offers art from the Renaissance period to today. 1934 Poplar Avenue, in Overton Park. Tel: (901) 722-3500.

"... the first of January 1832, the sun rising in a brilliant
revealed to us New Orleans across the masts of a thousand

—Alexis de ꟷ

New Orleans
Louisiana

Located on a crescent-shaped piece of land along the Mississippi River, New Orleans was once the swampy domain of alligators, snakes and mosquitoes. Founded in 1718 by the French and ceded to Spain in 1762, the town, surrounded by sugar plantations, grew into a major port city. When New Orleans became a territory of the United States in 1803, it was already a cosmopolitan town with a distinct French and Spanish tone. This unique culture attracts millions of visitors to the "Cresent City" each year.

This city relishes its cuisine and revels in good times. New Orleans fare, ranging from jambalaya—a rice dish with chicken, shrimp, tomatoes and sausage—to crawfish etouffeé—crawfish covered in a spicy tomato-based sauce—is a culinary mix of French, Spanish and African styles.

The city is perhaps most famous for its Mardi Gras festival, which begins on "Fat Tuesday" and continues for one week before the somber Ash Wednesday start of Lent. Mardi Gras is the most opulent celebration held in New Orleans, but visitors can find a celebration of some sort almost every day of the year.

Tocqueville and Beaumont spent most of the first three days of 1832 exploring the French Quarter. "Fine houses, huts; streets muddy and unpaved. Spanish architecture, flat English roofs. Bricks, small French doorways," Tocqueville wrote in his journal.

They rushed to discover all they could about New Orleans. "Population similarly mixed, faces of all shades of colour. Language French, English, Spanish, Creole," was how

A walk through the French Quarter leads visitors past historic houses covered with ornate ironwork and a dizzying array of cabarets, piano bars, restaurants and galleries.

New Orleans dock on the Mississippi River, 1850

145

New Orleans, Louisiana

...iginated in Africa, made its way to
...ne position of power in voodoo is
...Laveau, who rose to power in the
... voodoo queen. Born in the late 1700s,
...gitimate mulatto daughter of a wealthy
...eans were reported to have been terrified
... her voodoo charms. She is said to be
...tery No.1; her tombstone is frequently
... paraphernalia.

...described the throngs
in the streets.

They visited M.
Guillemin, a consul
for the French
government. He
talked to them about
how important it was
to keep the French
culture alive in New
Orleans. The consul
also reflected on the
growth of New
Orleans. "In the 15
years I have been
here, the prosperity
of the region has
increased an hundred fold. I have
seen the *quartiers* rear themselves
in the midst of
infested swamps,
palaces replace
cabins, the city
increase in
population ... the
future of Louisiana
is Wonderful."

The French
nobles attended a
quadroon ball. For
Tocqueville, it was a
disturbing sight.
"... all the men
white, all the women
coloured; or at least
of African blood.
Single tie created by
immorality between
the two races."

Cast iron balcony
in the historic
French Quarter

Strictly speaking,
Creoles, natives
of New Orleans,
are descendants
of early French or
Spanish settlers.
Cajuns, on the
other hand, are
descended from the
French Canadians
of New Acadia
(now Nova Scotia)
who were exiled by
the British in 1765
and settled in the
bayous and
swamps of South
Louisiana. "Cajun"
is a vernacular
pronunciation
of "Acadian."

What to See

Jackson Square
The heart of the French Quarter,
this square was originally a parade
ground. Located in the square is
St. Louis Cathedral, one of New
Orleans' oldest churches which
dates back to 1794.
615 pere Antoine Alley.
Tel: (504) 525-9585.

To the left of the cathedral is
the **Cabildo Building,** the state
house built in 1799 from which
the Spanish Governor ruled. It
features exhibits, artifacts and
historical documents.
701 Chartres Street.
Tel: (504) 568-6968.

To the right of the cathedral is
the **Presbytere** which was originally
built as a home for priests but never
used. It contains the Louisiana
State Museum's portrait gallery.
751 Chartres Street.
Tel: (504) 568-6968.

Hermann-Grima House
This restored house, completed in
1831, depicts the lifestyle of a
wealthy Creole family. Tours
include a look at the slave
quarters, the stables and a Creole
kitchen. Creole cooking
demonstrations are held every
Thursday, October through May.
820 St. Louis Street.
Tel: (504) 525-5661.

Mardi Gras King

Louisiana State Museum

The State Museum, housed in eight historic buildings throughout the French Quarter, offers a look at the city's traditions. Included in the museum are the **Pontalba Buildings** which flank **Jackson Square** and were erected by the Baroness Pontalba. The red brick buildings, built in 1849, were at one time the city's most desirable addresses. The lower building features an 1850s kitchen, parlor and servants quarters. St. Ann and St. Peter Streets. Tel: (504) 568-6968.

The **Old Mint** was the only building to serve as both a U.S. and a Confederate mint. The mint operated during most of the 19th century; production ceased in 1909. On the second floor are the **Jazz** and **Carnival Museums** which chronicle the musical and celebration traditions of New Orleans. 400 Esplanade Avenue. Tel: (504) 568-6968.

Historic New Orleans Collection

This 18th- and 19th-century complex of buildings contains a research center as well as changing exhibits about the history of the city and Louisiana. 533 Royal Street. Tel: (504) 523-4662.

New Orleans Historic Voodoo Museum

The museum features a vast collection of voodoo artifacts, with exhibits on various rituals. The museum also offers city walking tours and swamp tours. 724 Dumaine Street. Tel: (504) 523-7685.

Natchez Steamboat

This stern-wheeled steamboat offers two-hour narrated cruises along the Mississippi. Toulouse Street Wharf, near Jackson Square. Tel: (504) 586-8777.

New Orleans Today

New Orleans is more than a good-time city and it extends far beyond the **French Quarter**. The **Garden District**, which was originally developed as the settlement for Americans, also has many elegant homes. **Riverwalk,** along the Mississippi, at the foot of Poydras and Canal Streets, offers 200 shops, restaurants and cafés.

New Orleans has a population of more than 400,000 and is the second largest port in the United States. It is also a center of higher education and home to Tulane University, Loyola University, Xavier University and Dillard Univeristy.

French Quarter entertainer

147

Inns *and* Outs

How to get there:

From the north take I-59 to I-10 to downtown New Orleans. From the east/west take I-10 into the city.

Where to stay:

For lodging information contact the New Orleans Metropolitan Convention and Visitors Bureau. 1520 Sugar Bowl Drive, New Orleans, LA 70112. Tel: (504) 566-5011.

Other Attractions

City Park

1,500 acres include golf courses, tennis courts, boating, fishing and pony rides. The park contains the city's botanical gardens and the New Orleans Museum of Art. 1 Palm Drive. Tel: (504) 482-4888.

Old Absinthe House

Built in 1798-1806, this house became a popular barroom in 1826 and, except during Prohibition, has been one ever since. Blacksmith Jean Lafitte, who aided the Americans in the Battle of New Orleans, once had a secret room on the second floor where he stored contraband. 240 Bourbon Street, at Bienville Street. Tel: (504) 523-3181.

Aquarium of the Americas

Visitors will find more than 10,000 species of marine life at the Aquarium. There is a 400,000-gallon replica of the Gulf of Mexico on display as well as replicas of a Caribbean reef and a rain forest, complete with a waterfall. 1 Canal Street. Tel: (504) 581-4629.

Audubon Zoological Garden

More than 1,000 species of animals live here. Exhibits include a replica of the African Savanna, Australian Outback and the Asian Domain. 6500 Magazine Street. Tel: (504) 581-4629.

Kern's Mardi Gras World

Visitors can take guided tours of the workshops where the elaborate Mardi Gras floats are created. Mardi Gras costumes and props are also on display. 233 Newton Street. Tel: (504) 361-7821.

Longue Vue House and Gardens

Surrounded by acres of fountains and gardens, this Greek-Revival mansion was the home of Edgar Bloom Stern, a wealthy cotton broker, and his wife Edith. It is furnished with 18th- and 19th-century antiques. Guided tours are available. 7 Bamboo Road. Tel: (504) 488-5488.

Mobile
Alabama

Situated along the warm waters of Mobile Bay, the city charms visitors with its panoramic views of the bay, Spanish moss and wide oak-lined streets. Founded by the French and later controlled by the British and the Spanish, the city's architecture reflects its diverse heritage. The varied styles of the historic homes of Church Street, De Tonti Square, Government Street and Oakleigh Garden District are adorned with intricate iron work, reminiscent of French and Spanish influences, and white antebellum columns.

Mobile was the first American city to celebrate Mardi Gras. Legend has it that the first party was thrown shortly after the city was founded in 1702. Beginning at Thanksgiving each year and continuing until Ash Wednesday, the city celebrates with a series of balls and parades hosted by secret societies. The crowning of the King and Queen of Mardi Gras is the highlight of the season.

Tocqueville and Beaumont arrived in Mobile on January 4, 1832 in search of a stagecoach. With a population of 3,000, Mobile was starting to come into its own as a center for exporting cotton. Increasing numbers of merchants, laborers and tradesmen traveled in and out of the city.

Tocqueville and Beaumont were scheduled to return to France soon and were anxious to cover as much ground as possible. They discovered, however, that the stagecoach was filled. But, in the spirit of hospitality for which Mobile is known, two travelers gave up their seats and allowed Tocqueville and Beaumont to continue on their way.

The Civil War Battle of Mobile Bay was fought on August 5, 1864 and was won by Union forces. It was the first naval battle in the United States to utilize modern technology such as iron ships, explosive shells and mines.

Mobile's City Hall and New Market, 1857

149

What to See

Battleship Memorial Park

Visitors can tour a World War II submarine and explore the *USS Alabama*, a 35,000-ton warship which serves as a memorial to men and women of Alabama who fought in American wars. Other exhibits include a P-51 Mustang fighter plane and *Calamity Jane*, a B-52 bomber which houses a flight simulator that lets visitors experience a mock flight. 2703 Battleship Parkway, off I-10. Tel: (334) 433-2703.

Moon pies, soft chocolate-covered marshmallow cookies, are one of the prized trinkets thrown from floats during Mardi Gras.

Bellingrath Gardens and Home

Twenty miles south of Mobile lies Bellingrath, a mansion set on a 905-acre estate featuring one of the world's finest azalea gardens. In the spring more than 200 species of azaleas bloom. The house was built by Coca-Cola bottling pioneer Walter D. Bellingrath and contains an extensive collection of period furnishings, including fine china and porcelain. The *Southern Belle* riverboat, which departs from the estate, offers tours of the Fowl River. 12401 Bellingrath Gardens Road, Theodore. Tel: (334) 973-2217.

Museum of Mobile

This museum traces Mobile's past with artifacts and exhibits including a display of gowns once worn by the Queens of Mardi Gras, antique carriages and a collection of silver crafted by Mobile's premier silversmith James Conning. The *Slavery in Mobile* exhibit tells the stories of some of Mobile's urban and plantation African Americans. 355 Government Street. Tel: (334) 434-7569.

Condé-Charlotte Museum House

Built in 1822-24 as Mobile's first jail, this house reflects the periods of Mobile's diverse history. Rooms are furnished in French Empire, 18th-century English and American Federal styles. A walled, 18th-century Spanish garden surrounds the house. 104 Theatre Street. Tel: (334) 432-4722.

Oakleigh

This antebellum mansion was built in 1833. It was spared by Union troops during the war and became the center of Mobile society following the Civil War. Costumed guides give tours of the antique-furnished house. The

150 Bellingrath Gardens

Oakleigh House

mansion takes its name from the towering oak trees which surround it. 350 Oakleigh Place.
Tel: (334) 432-1281.

The Gunner's Room and Artillery Stores at Fort Conde

Fort Condé Mobile Visitor Welcome Center
A reconstructed French fort from the early 1700s featuring cannons, muskets and costumed soldiers, serves as Mobile's official welcome center. Artifacts unearthed during excavation are on display. 150 South Royal Street.
Tel: (334) 434-7304.

Mobile *Today*

Alabama's only seaport, Mobile has a population of more than 190,000. Mobile's shipping industry remains strong today. Millions of tons of cargo stream into the port every year. The city also has many recreational activities to offer such as golf and water sports. South of Mobile, near Gulf Shores, are miles of sandy white beaches.

Inns and Outs

How to get there:
From the north, take I-65 to Old Shell Road and head east. From the east/west, take I-10 into Mobile.

Where to stay:
For lodging information contact the Mobile Convention & Visitors Corporation.
One South Water Street, Mobile, AL 36602.
Tel: (334) 415-2000.

Other Attractions

Mobile Museum of Art
More than 4,000 works of art are housed here, including American landscapes and American art from the 1930s and 1940s. The museum also features contemporary arts and crafts as well as changing exhibits. 4850 Museum Drive.
Tel: (334) 343-2667.

Exploreum Museum of Science
Hands-on exhibits allow visitors to explore many of the principles of science. Exhibits focus on life, earth and physical science. 1906 Springhill Avenue.
Tel: (334) 476-6873.

Mobile is famous for its azaleas which were brought to the city in 1754. Each spring the city hosts the Azalea Trail Festival, which winds along a 35-mile trail through the city's floral-filled streets and historic buildings.

151

Montgomery
Alabama

Montgomery, the capital of Alabama, has been the setting for some of the most dramatic events in the history of the South. In 1861, the city became the first capital of the Confederate States of America. On April 11 of that year, a telegram with orders to fire on Charleston's Fort Sumter was sent from the capital, and the Civil War began.

Almost a century later, on December 1, 1955, a tired Montgomery seamstress named Rosa Parks refused to give up her seat on the bus to a white person; she was arrested. Martin Luther King, Jr., a local minister, organized a bus boycott that lasted a year and highlighted the civil rights movement.

Today Montgomery is known for producing textiles, Victorian-style furniture and livestock. When Tocqueville and Beaumont arrived in Montgomery on January 6, 1832, the town had not yet been named the state capital. It was an energetic, busy

> **M**ontgomery was the capital of the Confederacy for only a few months of 1861. In July of that year, the capital moved to Richmond, Virginia.

Montgomery's Market Street, circa 1850

Whistlin' Dixie

On the steps of the Montgomery State Capitol on February 18, 1861, Jefferson Davis was sworn in as President of the Confederate States of America. To celebrate, the Montgomery bandmasters transcribed a popular song that had never before been scored. The band performed it in the inaugural parade. The song was "Dixie." The catchy tune was composed by Daniel Decatur Emmett for a minstrel show in New York City. A staunch Northerner, Emmett never intended his song to become the battle anthem of the South.

center of cotton commerce and transportation. The streets were muddy and lined with a few buildings made of logs and some new brick structures.

The Frenchmen shared a stagecoach with a young lawyer from Montgomery. Tocqueville questioned him about universal suffrage. Tocqueville recorded the conversation because it was "stamped with much practical good sense." The lawyer said the people of Alabama often made poor voting decisions. The citizens often voted for politicians who flattered them, failing to elect more educated men. Sometimes the representatives could not read or write.

Tocqueville asked if this resulted in bad legislation. The lawyer told him no; less able politicians generally followed the lead of more skilled statesmen. Tocqueville pondered this and later wrote in *Democracy in America,* "...universal suffrage is by no means a guarantee of the wisdom of the popular choice." But at the same time, the French noble was certain in America, "society governs itself for itself. All power centers in its bosom, and scarcely an individual is to be met with who would venture to conceive or, still less, to express the idea of seeking it elsewhere."

What to See

Old Alabama Town

Three blocks of downtown Montgomery are a reconstructed village offering visitors a glimpse of 17th-century life in Alabama. The town includes the Ordeman-Shaw House built in the 1850s, a tavern, a doctor's office, a one-room schoolhouse, a drugstore, a cotton gin and more. Craftspeople demonstrate weaving, wood carving, spinning and other skills of the past. 301 Columbus Street. Tel: (334) 240-4500.

Fort Toulouse/Jackson Park National Historic Landmark

Native Americans first inhabited this area in approximately 5,000 B.C. Fort Jackson was built here by Andrew Jackson in 1814. The park contains an Indian burial mound, an arboretum, a museum and "living history" reenactments every third weekend of the month. 2521 West Fort Toulouse Road, off US Highway 231, Wetumpka. Tel: (334) 567-3002.

The Civil Rights Memorial, on the corner of Washington Avenue and Hull Street, depicts key events in the civil rights movement and lists the names of 40 people who gave their lives for racial equality. It was designed by Maya Lin, the creator of the Vietnam Veterans Memorial in Washington, DC.

First White House of the Confederacy

First White House of the Confederacy

Jefferson Davis and his family lived here when Montgomery was the capital of the Confederacy. The house contains period furnishings and many of the Davis family's personal belongings, war relics and paintings.
644 Washington Avenue.
Tel: (334) 242-1861.

Montgomery's Visitors Center, located on the corner of Madison Avenue and North Hull Street in an 1850s antebellum mansion, offers tourist information and runs a free film about Montgomery.

Dexter Avenue King Memorial Baptist Church

The first pulpit of Reverend Martin Luther King, Jr., this church played a critical role in the Montgomery bus boycott and the ensuing struggle for civil rights. A mural entitled *The Beginning of a Dream* depicts King's civil rights fight from Montgomery to Memphis. 454 Dexter Avenue.
Tel: (334) 263-3970.

Betsy Ann Riverboat

This stern-wheel riverboat offers visitors a look at Montgomery from the Alabama River. Riverfront Park at the foot of Commerce Street.
Tel: (334) 265-7739.

State Archives and History Museum

This museum chronicles Alabama history with a series of exhibits focusing on Native Americans, military history, a portrait gallery and a children's gallery. 624 Washington Avenue.
Tel: (334) 242-4363.

Alabama State Capitol

Built in 1850-51, this pristine white capitol has been the seat of the state government for more than a century. Jefferson Davis took his oath of office here as President of the Confederate States of America.
600 Dexter Avenue.
Tel: (334) 242-3935.

Montgomery
Today

Located in central Alabama along the Alabama River, Montgomery has a population of more than 190,000. The capital city has a focus on higher education and the arts. Auburn

Dexter Avenue King Memorial Baptist Church

Alabama State Capitol

University at Montgomery and Alabama State University are among the institutions of higher education located here. The Alabama Shakespeare Festival runs from mid-November to late August and presents classical and modern plays performed in the 750-seat Festival Stage and the 225-seat Octagon. Maxwell Air Force Base was once the location of the Wright Brothers flight training school. Today it is the site of the Air Force's Air University.

Inns *and* Outs

How to get there:
From the north/south take I-65 to Montgomery. From the east/west take US Highway 80.

Where to stay:
For lodging information contact the Montgomery Visitors Center. 401 Madison Avenue, Montgomery, AL 36104. Tel: (334) 262-0013.

Other Attractions

Jasmine Hill Gardens
This 20-acre garden, landscaped with statues, fountains and pools, is modeled after Olympian Greece. A replica of the ruins of the Temple of Hera and avenues of flowering azaleas adorn the park. Guided tours are available. Jasmine Hill Road, off US Highway 231. Tel: (334) 567-6463.

Montgomery Museum of Fine Arts
This museum houses 19th- and 20th-century collections of American art. Also included is a hands-on children's exhibit. 1 Museum Drive. Tel: (334) 224-5700.

F. Scott and Zelda Fitzgerald Museum
The famous jazz-age writer, F. Scott Fitzgerald, and his wife, Zelda, lived here from 1931 to 1932. Zelda, whom Fitzgerald had met while stationed here during the waning days of World War I, was a native of Montgomery. The house contains paintings by Zelda as well as letters and photographs detailing the life of the famous couple. The museum also features a 25-minute video presentation. 919 Felder Avenue. Tel: (334) 264-4222.

Look for the C-SPAN plaque in front of the House of Mayors (c. 1853). The site is now commonly known as the United Way House. 532 South Perry Street.

155

Knoxville & Macon
Georgia

In Macon each spring, 224,000 Yoshino cherry trees bloom in an array of creamy white and pink colors. The city celebrates with a cherry blossom festival featuring more than 300 events.

C-SPAN's plaque for the Knoxville community has been placed at the Crawford County Courthouse in Roberta, Georgia, on US Highway 80.

A hot air balloonfest, parades, concerts, fireworks, amusement rides, arts and crafts displays, and tours of Macon's historic mansions take place during the week-long celebration.

Macon is steeped in Southern tradition. White columns and wide front porches embellish Macon's pre-Civil War mansions. The cotton industry created many of the town's fortunes and provided the capital to build the mansions.

When Tocqueville and Beaumont arrived in early January of 1832, the town was a major center for cotton trade and had a population of more than 2,000. They probably came through town by way of the Federal Road which was completed in 1811 and stretched from a point near Mobile, Alabama to Milledgeville, Georgia. Today Macon's Cotton Avenue incorporates part of the old road.

After leaving Macon, Tocqueville and Beaumont traveled through Knoxville, Georgia, a small town thirty miles west of Macon. Today the town has approximately thirty residents.

Tocqueville wrote that it was a "fascinating but very fatiguing journey, accompanied each day by the thousand annoyances that have been pursuing us for the last two months: carriages broken and overturned, bridges carried away, rivers swollen, no room in the stage; there are the ordinary events of our life."

Macon's Main Street, 1850

Making of the Texas Flag

In 1835, thirty-two men from Macon set out to help Texas in its struggle for independence against Mexico. Along the way, many new recruits joined the band. When the group stopped in Knoxville, Georgia, Joanna Troutman, a 17-year-old girl, presented the men with a white banner decorated with a single blue star in the center. Carried all the way from Georgia, the banner went on to become the famous Lone Star Flag of Texas.

What to See

Old Cannonball House and Macon Confederate Museum

The house acquired its name when it was hit by a Union cannonball on July 30, 1864. Visitors can still see the cannonball on the site where it landed. The Greek-Revival mansion contains period furnishings. A Confederate Museum is located in the former servants' quarters and contains artifacts from the War Between the States.
856 Mulberry Street, Macon.
Tel: (912) 745-5982.

Macon Museum of Arts and Sciences

The museum houses a collection of fossils, including whale skeletons discovered near Macon—the area was once at the edge of a prehistoric sea—nature trails and a planetarium. 4182 Forsyth Road, Macon. Tel: (912) 477-3232.

Harriet Tubman African American Museum

The museum's seven galleries are dedicated to preserving the history and culture of African Americans, with a special focus on those from Macon. There is an exhibition on inventions and discoveries made by African Americans and a wall mural—*From Africa to America*.
340 Walnut Street, Macon.
Tel: (912) 743-8544.

Woodruff House

Built in 1836, this mansion has been owned by Macon's most prominent citizens, including banker and railroad magnate Jerry Cowles. During the Civil War, the house was used as headquarters by both Confederate and Union forces. 988 Bond Street, Macon. Tel: (912) 744-2715.

Sidney's Tours of Historic Macon

Visitors can explore historic Macon with tours conducted by a Sidney Lanier costumed guide. Lanier was one of Georgia's most famous poets. Terminal Station, 200 Cherry Street, Macon. Tel: (912) 743-3401.

Hay House

Completed in 1859, this 24-room Italian Renaissance-Revival mansion is an exquisite expression of wealth. The house was built by William B. Johnston with all the modern amenities of the time including an indoor elevator, a ventilating system and intricate plumbing. The house features stunning stained-glass windows and hand-painted faux marble walls. 934 Georgia Avenue, Macon. Tel: (912) 742-8155.

The Hay House

Cherry Blossom Festival

Macon Today

For information about the Cherry Blossom Festival, contact Festival Events and Riding Tours at (912) 751-7429.

More than 100,000 people live in Macon today. The town is home to both Mercer University and Wesleyan College, the world's first university chartered specifically to grant degrees to women. Industry includes Brown and Williamson Tobacco Corporation, Cherokee Brick and Tile Company and Purina Mills Incorporated.

Inns and Outs

How to get there:
From Atlanta, go south on I-75 and take exit 53. Head east on I-16 and follow exit 2 or 4 to downtown.

Where to stay:
For lodging information contact the Macon-Bibb County

Convention and Visitors Bureau. 200 Cherry Street. Tel: (800) 768-3401 or (912) 743-3401. Also try the Greater Macon Chamber of Commerce. 305 Coliseum Drive, Macon, GA 31201. Tel: (912) 741-8000.

Other Attractions

Ocmulgee National Monument
This archaeological park interprets the various cultures of the native people who made their home here 10,000 years ago. The park features a reconstructed 1,000-year-old ceremonial earthlodge, a burial mound, temple mound, prehistoric trenches and a trading post used during colonial times.
1207 Emery Highway, Macon. Tel: (912) 752-8257.

Georgia Music Hall of Fame
This museum traces Georgia's rich musical heritage with exhibits on jazz, gospel and rock-and-roll. With its indoor model of a Georgia town, the Music Hall of Fame features concert videos, memorabilia, instruments, photos and listening rooms.
200 M. L. King Jr. Boulevard, Macon. Tel: (912) 750-8555.

Sidney Lanier Cottage
The birthplace of poet Sidney Lanier, this 1840s Victorian house is filled with period antiques and is the headquarters for the Middle Georgia Historical Society. 935 High Street, Macon. Tel: (912) 743-3851.

Georgia Music Hall of Fame

Milledgeville
Georgia

Milledgeville is a college town situated in the heart of Georgia, at the southern tip of Lake Sinclair along the Oconee River. Georgia College and State University, with its red brick and white-column buildings, as well as Georgia Military College, with its Gothic-style architecture, are both located in the center of town. Grand old houses in Federal and Victorian styles grace many of the streets. Inspired by Savannah, Georgia and Washington, DC, Milledgeville was founded and carefully planned in 1803 as Georgia's capital city.

Milledgeville served as the capital until 1868. It was here that Georgia voted to secede from the Union in 1861. Three years later, Union General William T. Sherman led his troops through town, burning down most of the government buildings and archives.

When Tocqueville traveled through Milledgeville in January of 1832, it was the political center of Georgia. From 1817 to 1868, the Georgia State Prison was located in the center of town. Tocqueville made no mention of the penitentiary and only named Milledgeville as a town he traveled through on his rapid stagecoach journey to Washington, DC. He described the trip as one in which he had to "dine on corn and pig, eat little, much, not at all... bed on the floor and sleep with one's clothes on; pass in a week from ice to heat and from heat to ice; put one's shoulder to the wheel or wake up in a ditch..."

Stetson-Sanford House

Sweet Silence

On their march to the sea, Union General William T. Sherman's troops stopped in Milledgeville in November, 1864. They stabled their horses in St. Stephen's Episcopal Church and poured molasses down the church's organ pipes to prevent them from being used to signal confederate sympathizers. St. Stephen's, built in 1841, stands at 200 South Wayne Street and is open to visitors.

What to See

Stetson-Sanford House

The headquarters of the Old Capital Historical Society, this Federal-style house was built by John Marlor in 1825. It contains intricate woodcarvings and ornate detailing and has received national acclaim for architectural design. Appointments are necessary for tours which can be arranged through the Convention and Visitors Bureau. Corner of Jackson and West Hancock Streets. Tel: (800) 653-1804.

> Local lore has it that pecans, one of Georgia's famous crops, were first grown in Milledgeville.

Old Governor's Mansion

Built in 1838, this Greek-Revival mansion once served as the home for nine of Georgia's governors during the days when Milledgeville was the state capital. Today it is the office of the president of Georgia College and State University and is open for guided tours. 120 South Clark Street. Tel: (912) 445-4545.

Historic Guided Trolley Tour

This tour gives visitors an overview of historic Milledgeville and includes stops at the Governor's Mansion and the Stetson-Sanford House. Tours depart from the Convention and Visitors Bureau at 200 West Hancock Street. Tel: (800) 653-1804.

John Marlor Arts Center

This Federal-style house with its tall portico was built in the 1830s. It houses the Milledgeville-Baldwin County Allied Arts and Elizabeth Marlor Bethune Art Gallery. 201 North Wayne Street. Tel: (912) 452-3950.

Museum and Archives of Georgia Education

This museum documents the history of Georgia's educational system and includes a replica of an early 20th-century classroom. The museum also houses many historic documents, photographs and artifacts. 131 South Clark Street. Tel: (912) 453-4391.

160 Old Governor's Mansion

Milledgeville Today

Milledgeville has a population of approximately 18,000. Georgia College and State University, a liberal arts college with about 5,500 students, and Georgia Military College, a coeducational junior college, are important centers of learning in the area. Central State Hospital, established in 1837, is located here and is one of the state's oldest mental health hospitals. Every fall the town hosts the Brown's Crossing Craftsmen Fair where artisans demonstrate crafts from yesteryear including leather making, quilting, weaving and metal work.

Inns and Outs

How to get there:
From Atlanta take I-20 to exit 51 at Madison; then take Highway 441 into Milledgeville. From Macon take Highway 129 to Route 22 into town.

Where to stay:
For lodging information contact the Milledgeville-Baldwin County Convention and Visitors Bureau. 200 West Hancock Street, Milledgeville, GA 31061. Tel: (800) 653-1804.

Other Attractions

Flannery O'Connor Memorial Room
Flannery O'Connor, acclaimed Southern writer, spent much of her life in Milledgeville and attended school at Georgia Women's College, now Georgia College and State University. The university operates this room which is furnished in the Victorian-style of the 1870s and contains many of the writer's belongings. Dillard Russell Library, Georgia College and State University. Tel: (912) 445-4047

Lake Sinclair
This 15,330-acre lake was created in 1953 with the completion of the Sinclair Dam. It stretches across 417 miles of shoreline and is a prime fishing, swimming and water sports area.

Lockerly Arboretum
Forty-five acres of a former plantation are landscaped with a wide variety of plants, trees and flowers. Guided tours are available. 1534 Irwinton Road. Tel: (912) 452-2112.

Lockerly Arboretum

Milledgeville, Georgia

Augusta
Georgia

Located along the Savannah River, Augusta is the oldest and second largest city in Georgia. Established in 1735 as an Indian trading post, the settlement grew quickly. Tocqueville and Beaumont passed through Augusta on their Southern sweep in January of 1832.

When the French nobles arrived, the town had a population of about 7,000 people and, as a center for inland cotton trading, was booming. Augusta was making advances—fresh water had just been piped into town, the streets were planted with trees and attending the theater was a favorite diversion.

Sixty years later Augusta, with its mild climate and beautiful scenery, was discovered by the wealthy families of the North and became a favored resort. Grand houses and resort hotels were built to accommodate the lodging demand.

One popular hotel constructed a nine-hole course for the new Scottish game of golf. The sport caught on and in 1933, legendary golfer Bobby Jones founded the Augusta National Golf Club, which later became the site of the Masters Golf Tournament. Each April, Augusta continues the tradition and the golf world flocks to the city.

The town still retains glimpses of its past. Despite a devastating fire in 1916, Broad Street, Augusta's historic commercial district, is lined with many 19th-century buildings. Many of the old resort homes remain in the hills of the Summerville neighborhood.

> The Confederate Monument, a tall marble obelisk, stands at the 700 block of Broad Street. It was erected in 1878 by the Ladies Memorial Association to honor Civil War soldiers.

162

The Court House, Medical College and First Presbyterian Church, 1840

Augusta, Georgia

Haunted Pillar

From the 1830s until 1878, a farmer's market stood at the intersection of Broad and Fifth Streets. Augusta legend has it that a traveling preacher was once denied permission to proselytize in the market square. Angry, he told the people that the market would be destroyed as punishment. On February 7, a rare tornado devastated the market. It was never rebuilt, and all that remains is a tall dark pillar on the sidewalk of Broad and Fifth Streets.

The Haunted Pillar

What to See

Augusta-Richmond County Museum

This museum depicts the history of Augusta from times when Native Americans roamed the sandy hills above the Savannah River through the Revolutionary and Civil Wars. Collections include exhibits on Native Americans, the railroad and other aspects of the Augusta area. Situated along the Riverwalk. 560 Reynolds Street.
Tel: (706) 722-8454.

Ezekiel Harris House

This Federal-style house once housed tobacco merchants while they were in town selling their crops. The house was built in 1797 by Ezekiel Harris, a wealthy tobacco merchant. The Harris House is furnished with antiques and displays archaeological artifacts found on the grounds. 1822 Broad Street.
Tel: (706) 724-0436.

Morris Museum of Art

More than 2,500 works by Southern artists are displayed here. The collection spans over 200 years and also features changing exhibits.
10th Street and Riverwalk.
Tel: (706) 724-7501.

Cotton Exchange Museum and Welcome Center

Built in 1886 as the headquarters of Georgia's booming cotton trade, this museum takes visitors back to the time when cotton was king. The museum features antique plows, tickertape machines and a 45-foot-wide wooden blackboard with early 20th-century cotton prices chalked on it.
32 8th Street.
Tel: (706) 724-4067.

Historic Cotton Welcome Center and Museum

The Jessye Norman Amphitheater at Riverwalk

Riverwalk

On the shores of the Savannah, Augusta's Riverwalk, bordered with trees and flowers, winds past gardens and scenic bulwarks extending out over the water. Restaurants, antique stores and museums line the walk. The 1,600-seat Riverwalk Amphitheater, which overlooks the Savannah, plays host to various national performances.

Gertrude Herbert Institute of Art

Built in 1818 for Georgia statesman Nicholas Ware, the house was referred to as "Ware's Folly" because of its high construction cost. Today it showcases changing art exhibits. 506 Telfair Street. Tel: (706) 722-5495.

Boating is a popular Augusta pastime. Each March, the Invitational Rowing Regatta and Regatta Fest is held on the Savannah River; later in the year, motorboat and dragboat races are held.

Meadow Garden

Built in the late 1700s, this is one of the oldest houses in Augusta. It was the home of George Walton, the youngest signer of the Declaration of Independence and is furnished with period pieces. 1320 Independence Drive. Tel: (706) 724-4174.

Augusta Today

With a population of more than 40,000, the city is home to the Medical College of Georgia, Augusta State University and Paine College. Textile manufacturing and cotton trading still play a role in the commercial life of Augusta. Procter & Gamble, Federal Paperboard, and Amoco are also located in the city. The main newspaper, *The Augusta Chronicle,* is the oldest newspaper in the South.

Inns and Outs

How to get there:

From Columbia, South Carolina, take I-20 west to exit 66. From the exit take River Watch Parkway and follow the parkway to downtown.

Where to stay:

For lodging information contact the Augusta Metropolitan Convention and Visitors Bureau. 32 8th Street, Augusta, GA 30901. Tel: (706) 823-6600 or (800) 726-0243.

Other Attractions

Fort Discovery

This museum is devoted to exploring the mysteries of science and offers hands-on exhibits for children, teachers and adults. Visitors can virtually walk on the moon, paint with lasers and spin a gravity-defying, 1,000-pound floating stone on their fingers. Located on the Riverwalk at 7th and Reynolds Streets. Tel: (800) 325-5445.

164

Columbia
South Carolina

Located in the heart of South Carolina, Columbia was founded as the state capital in 1786. In 1865, when General William Sherman's troops occupied Columbia, a massive fire swept through the city, destroying three-fourths of its structures.

A few antebellum mansions remain standing on Columbia's wide shady streets, and the city retains a genteel southern ambiance. At the same time, as the home of the University of South Carolina's main campus and the site of U.S. Army base Fort Jackson, it is a thriving educational and military center.

When Tocqueville and Beaumont passed through Columbia in January of 1832, the city had a population of 7,000. On January 12, the two travelers met up with an old acquaintance, Joel Roberts Poinsett, the former United States ambassador to Mexico. The two had met Poinsett in Philadelphia. Poinsett was also traveling by stagecoach from South Carolina to Washington, DC on the same route as the French nobles.

Tocqueville took the opportunity to ask Poinsett a series of questions. He was curious about presidential elections, the upkeep of roads in America—he had suffered through a number of accidents caused by bad roads—and about the power of America's shipping fleet. Poinsett offered his opinions on all of those subjects. He told Tocqueville that American sailors were the most industrious in the world, not only because they were paid higher wages than sailors from other nations, but because they were independent, capable men.

Poinsett foresaw America emerging as the maritime leader of the world. It was a conversation Tocqueville took to heart. He later wrote in *Democracy in America,*

On his return to the United States from Mexico, Poinsett introduced the country to the vivid flower that was named for him, the poinsettia.

A panorama of Columbia in 1854

Walking on the Wide Side

On March 22, 1786, the South Carolina General Assembly decided to create a new state capital. The site of Columbia was chosen along the Congaree River. The avenues were laid out to be 100 feet wide. The width was chosen in an effort to promote better air quality and deter malaria. Malaria had not yet been connected with the mosquito and a common belief was that malaria was caused by swamp or river gases.

"When I contemplate the ardor with which the Anglo-Americans prosecute commerce, the advantages which aid them, and the success of their undertakings, I cannot help believing that they will one day become the foremost maritime power of the globe. They are born to rule the seas, as the Romans were to conquer the world."

In 1936, the Big Apple Night Club, a popular African-American dance club, was located in an old Jewish synagogue on 1000 Hampton Street. The "Big Apple Dance," which was popular in the 1930s was born here. Today the Big Apple is used for special events.

What to See

South Carolina State Museum

Housed in the world's first electronic mill, the State Museum chronicles the art, history, science and technology of South Carolina. The museum features collections of South Carolina art, a historical exhibit featuring a one-room school and hands-on science and technology exhibits.
301 Gervais Street.
Tel: (803) 737-4921.

Robert Mills House

This 1823 house was designed by Robert Mills, the first federal architect of the United States and the designer of the Washington Monument. The house features a decorative arts collection and is surrounded by English-style gardens.
1616 Blanding Street.
Tel: (803) 252-1770.

Woodrow Wilson's Boyhood Home

President Woodrow Wilson's parents designed this house. Wilson lived here from 1872-74. The house is furnished with Wilson family memorabilia and the bed in which Woodrow Wilson was born.
1705 Hampton Street.
Tel: (803) 252-1770.

McKissick Museum

Located on the campus of the University of South Carolina, this museum focuses on regional history and folklore and features changing art exhibits.
USC Horseshoe.
Tel: (803) 777-7251.

State House

One of the few buildings to survive Sherman's destruction, the State House was started in 1855 and finally completed in 1900. Six bronze stars mark the spots where Union artillery shells hit the walls.
Main and Gervais Streets.
Tel: (803) 734-2430.

166 State Capitol

Columbia skyline

Mann-Simons Cottage
This cottage is the 1850s home of Celia Mann, a former slave who, upon gaining her freedom, walked 100 miles from Charleston to Columbia. She became an important mid-wife for city residents. The house features original Mann-Simons family furniture, horse-hair plaster walls and authentic, 19th-century tools of midwifery.
1403 Richland Street.
Tel: (803) 252-1770.

Columbia
Today
Fort Jackson, the Army's largest training center with approximately 97,000 soldiers, civilian employees, retirees and family members, is located here. Columbia is also home to the University of South Carolina which was chartered in 1801. The capital city has a population of more than 100,000.

Inns and Outs

How to get there:
From the north, take 95 south to I-20 west. Follow to I-77 south which leads to Columbia. From the south, head east on I-20 to I-77 south.

Where to stay:
For lodging information contact the Columbia Metropolitan Visitors Center.

1012 Gervais Street,
Columbia, SC 29201.
Tel: (800) 264-4884.

Other Attractions

Columbia Museum of Art
The museum displays Baroque, Medieval and Renaissance paintings as well as a collection of 19th- and 20th-century paintings, decorative arts and sculptures. Corner of Main and Hampton Streets.
Tel: (803) 799-2810.

Riverbanks Zoological Park and Botanical Garden
Ranked among one of the top zoos in the nation, Riverbanks is home to more than 2,000 animals. Across from the zoo, on the west bank of the Saluda River, visitors can explore 70 acres of woodlands and gardens. 500 Wildlife Parkway, off I-26 at Greystone Boulevard.
Tel: (803) 779- 8717.

Cayce Historical Museum
A short distance from Columbia, this museum traces the history of the South Carolina midlands from trading post days to the early 1900s. 1800 12th Street Extension, Cayce.
Tel: (803) 796-9020.

Riverfront Park at Laurel and Gist Streets centers around the city's old waterworks. A walkway leads to the Columbia Canal which was built between 1819 and 1824 and features old brick buildings and wrought-iron fencing.

167

Fayetteville
NorthCarolina

Fayetteville has been a center for defense-related activities since 1836 when Congress set aside funds to build a major arsenal in the city. During the Civil War, the armory produced 10,000 weapons including the Fayetteville rifle for Confederate troops. Today Fayetteville, located along the scenic Cape Fear River in southeastern North Carolina, is home to Pope Air Force Base and Fort Bragg, the home of the Airborne and Special Operations Forces. It has a military population of 45,000.

A fter returning to France from his nine-month stay in America, Beaumont married Clementine de Lafayette, the Marquis de Lafayette's granddaughter.

Fayetteville is named for the Revolutionary War hero General Marquis de Lafayette of France. In 1825, Lafayette made a triumphant return to the United States. He toured many of the same cities that Tocqueville and Beaumont later visited. On March 4, the town's Independent Light Infantry ushered the General into town with great fanfare where hundreds of citizens greeted him.

To this day the town still honors its namesake. A bronze bust of Lafayette stands under Market House and an eight-foot statue stands in Cross Creek Park.

When Tocqueville and Beaumont arrived in Fayetteville in January of 1832, the city was recovering from a devastating fire. What started out as a small kitchen fire in May of 1831 ravaged the town, destroying more than 600 buildings. The Sandford House, the Oval Ballroom and the Baker-Haigh-Nimocks House on Fayetteville's Heritage Square are three examples of the few houses that survived the great fire.

What to See

Museum of the Cape Fear Historical Complex
This museum traces the history of southeastern North Carolina from Native-American times to the early 20th century with exhibits and artifacts including antique firearms, toys and a replica of a country store. 801 Arsenal Avenue. Tel: (910) 486-1330.

82nd Division War Memorial Airborne Museum
More than 3,000 artifacts collected from World War I through the Gulf War are on display here. Artifacts include weapons, helmets, uniforms and other paraphernalia. Building C-6841, corner of Ardennes and Gela Streets. Tel: (910) 432-3443.

168 Statue of Lafayette

Finding His Name and His Game

In March 1914, at the age of 19, George Herman Ruth traveled to Fayetteville, North Carolina with the Baltimore Orioles—a minor league team at that time—for spring training. It was here that the world-famous baseball player hit his first professional home run and, due to his youth, acquired his nickname, "Babe."

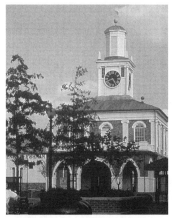

The Market House, built in 1832

Market House

The old market building, which was built in 1832, stands as a symbol of Fayetteville. It once housed the town's art museum and, later, the National Bank. Bordered by Hay, Gillespie, Person and Green Streets. Tel: (910) 483-2073.

Fayetteville Independent Light Infantry Armory and Museum

The second oldest active militia unit in the United States operates this museum which houses documents, uniforms and artifacts. Open by appointment. 210 Burgess Street. Tel: (910) 481-3510.

Fort Bragg

For a tour of the base stop by the Fort Bragg Visitors Center. Building 8, 5476 2nd Street. (910) 396-8687.

John F. Kennedy Special Warfare Center

Visitors delve into warfare history through the military artifacts and cultural items on display. The collection focuses on the United States special forces. Ardennes and Reilly Streets. Tel: (910) 432-4272.

Fayetteville Today

Thousands of soldiers, airmen and civilians are employed at Fort Bragg; but the town is also the seat of Fayetteville State University and Methodist College. Cape Fear Valley Medical Center and the Womack Army Medical Center are located here as well. Fayetteville has a population of nearly 80,000.

Inns and Outs

How to get there:

From Raleigh take I-40 south to I-95 south. Take exit 56 several miles to downtown Person Street.

Where to stay:

For lodging information contact the Fayetteville Area Convention and Visitors Bureau. 245 Person Street, Fayetteville, NC 28301. Tel: (910) 483-5311 or (888) NC-CHARM.

Look for the C-SPAN plaque in the plaza beneath the Market House. This historic building is bordered by Hay, Gillespie, Person and Green Streets.

169

Norfolk
Virginia

Norfolk's busy Waterside Festival Marketplace, situated along the downtown harbor, is a delightful place to absorb some of the city's nautical ambiance. Boutiques, restaurants and galleries line the waterfront. From here, visitors can board the *Spirit of Norfolk* for cruises on Norfolk's historic waterways.

Located at the mouth of the Chesapeake Bay, Norfolk's 45-foot-deep channel accommodates even the largest freighters. Shipping has been the life blood of the city since the 1700s when boats from Europe and the West Indies filled its deep harbor. By the end of the century, Norfolk was known as the colonies' most prosperous city.

Today, the maritime tradition continues as Norfolk is recognized as a key international port. Norfolk Naval Base is the world's largest naval complex and is home to the United States Atlantic Fleet which harbors more than 100 ships.

Tocqueville and Beaumont came to Norfolk on January 15, 1832 in search of passage to Washington, DC. Beaumont wrote that their arrival in Virginia marked the beginning of the end of their 'great American journey.' They had been traveling for close to nine months and had only a few weeks left in the United States.

At the turn of the century, Norfolk was a booming trade center. When the French nobles arrived, however, the city was recovering from the strict trade embargoes which the British had enforced during the War of 1812. The two men stayed in Norfolk only one night. The next day they boarded a steamer and set off for the nation's capital.

At the 1904 World's Fair in St. Louis, Norfolk resident Abe Doumar is said to have introduced the world to the ice cream cone. Today ice cream cones are still served at Doumar's Drive-In Restaurant, located on 1919 Monticello Avenue and operated by the Doumar family.

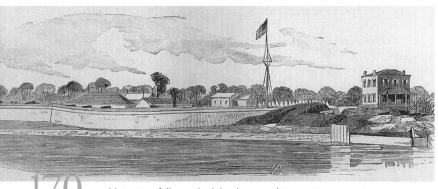

170

Old Fort Norfolk was built by the United States Government and later strengthened by the Confederates

Norfolk, Virginia

The Battle of the Ironclads

On March 9, 1862, across from the shores of Norfolk in the James River, the first battle between Union and Confederate ironclad ships was waged. The naval fight is often called the Battle of the *Monitor* and the *Merrimack*. But the *Monitor* never actually fought the *Merrimack*. Instead the *U.S.S. Monitor* fired against the *C.S.S. Virginia*. The wooden *Merrimack* was an abandoned Union ship that Confederate forces salvaged from the Norfolk naval yard. The Southern forces forged the iron themselves, encased the ship in armor and rechristened her the *C.S.S. Virginia*.

What to See

Historic Fort Norfolk

In 1794, George Washington authorized the construction of several forts along American harbors. Fort Norfolk is one of the last to remain standing. During the War of 1812, the fort acted as a key defense for Norfolk's inner harbor. Battle reenactments are staged here throughout the year, and the fort is open to the public on weekdays. Guided tours are available by appointment. Located on the banks of the Elizabeth River at 810 Front Street. Tel: (757) 625-1720.

Norfolk Naval Base

Narrated bus tours of the naval station, air station, submarine piers and waterfront are offered. 9079 Hampton Boulevard, Suite 100. Tel: (757) 444-7955.

The Moses Myers House

Built in 1792 for Moses Myers, one of the nation's first millionaires, and his family, the house contains family furnishings as well as paintings by Gilbert Stuart and Thomas Sully. The house is one of the few in the nation with exhibits on the traditions of early Jewish settlers. 331 Bank Street. Tel: (757) 664-6200.

St. Paul's Church

Norfolk's oldest building, St. Paul's survived the burning of the city by the British on New Year's Day, 1776. The church still has some scars, including a cannonball that remains lodged in the southeastern wall. A Tiffany stained-glass window adorns the church. Guided tours are available upon request. 201 St. Paul's Boulevard. Tel: (757) 627-4353.

Chrysler Museum

More than 30,000 pieces of art, including a collection of Tiffany glass, photography, paintings and sculptures from all over the world, are housed in this waterfront museum. 245 West Olney Road. Tel: (757) 664-6200.

The Waterside Festival Marketplace & Marina

THE MACARTHUR MEMORIAL

The Douglas MacArthur Memorial

MacArthur's life is shown in the Memorial Theater. MacArthur's tomb lies in Norfolk's 1850s City Hall rotunda. MacArthur Square, bordered by City Hall Avenue and Bank Street. Tel: (757) 441-2965.

The *Spirit of Norfolk*
The *Spirit of Norfolk,* which offers a two-hour cruise of the Norfolk waterways, departs from the Waterside Festival Marketplace. Tel: (757) 627-7771.

General Douglas MacArthur Memorial
"Old soldiers never die; they just fade away," stated Douglas MacArthur in his farewell address to Congress. Visitors can see his tomb as well as the General's trademark cap, sunglasses and corncob pipe in this museum, which traces the life and career of the World War II hero. The museum also features photographs and paintings. A film depicting

The National Maritime Center-Nauticus
On the waterfront in downtown Norfolk, this huge attraction houses a science center, an aquarium and an interactive museum with virtual attractions that allow you to land a jet fighter on a carrier, sail a boat or fight a naval battle. The center also features a giant-screened version of the Academy Award nominated film, "The Living Sea." 1 Waterside Drive. Tel: (800) 664-1080.

1/2 Nauticus, the National Maritime Center

Norfolk skyline

Norfolk
Today

The city of more than 250,000 residents has several historic districts. The Freemason District on the city's west side has streets paved with stones that were once used as ship ballast. The Ghent District, which borders Old Dominion University, contains many restaurants and boutiques. In April, the city hosts the International Azalea Festival in honor of the NATO Alliance. The city's industry includes ship repair, international shipping services, trucking and the Norfolk Southern Corporation railway company.

Inns and Outs

How to get there:
From Washington, DC, take I-95 south to I-295 and then to I-64. Then take I-564 to the Naval Base or to downtown.

Where to stay:
For lodging information contact the Norfolk Convention and Visitors Bureau. 232 East Main Street, Norfolk, VA 23510. Tel: (800) 368-3097.

Other Attractions

Hermitage Foundation Museum
The museum houses a collection of Western and Asian art. 7637 North Shore Road. Tel: (757) 423-2052.

Hunter House Victorian Museum
Once the home of Dr. J.W. Hunter, this house displays a collection of Victorian furnishings including toys and an early collection of 20th-century medical equipment. 240 West Freemason Street. Tel: (757) 623-9814.

Norfolk Botanical Gardens
More than 100 acres of gardens including azaleas, other rhododendrons, camellias and roses can be explored by foot, a trackless train or canal boat. The Tropical Pavilion showcases more than 100 varieties of rare and tropical plants. 6700 Azalea Garden Road. Tel: (757) 664-6879.

Look for the C-SPAN plaque at the Moses Myers House. 331 Bank Street.

173

"Washington offers the sight of an arid plain, burned by the sun, on which are scattered two or three sumptuous edifices..."

—Alexis de Tocqueville

Washington DC

Today, the domed Capitol, set high on a hill, provides a view that looks out over the green expanse of the National Mall toward the Washington Monument, the Reflecting Pool, the Lincoln Memorial and the Potomac River. Pierre L'Enfant, the French engineer who designed the capital, planned the broad vistas and monumental buildings to highlight the city's power. Washington, the seat of American government and a cosmopolitan city, serves as headquarters to many national and international organizations, corporations and lobbying firms.

When Tocqueville and Beaumont arrived here in late January of 1832, the capital was a muddy city of 2,000 people.

"This town, whose population is inconsiderable, is yet immense in area. Distances are almost as great as in Paris. The consequence is that the houses are scattered here and there, without connection between...Outside of the fact that it makes a very ugly panorama, it's very annoying for those with visits to make," wrote Beaumont.

The Frenchmen had many people to call upon. During their three-week stay, Tocqueville and Beaumont were honored by Washington society. A ball attended by more than three hundred people was held in their honor; Congressmen and ambassadors never ceased to issue invitations to the esteemed travelers.

> Tocqueville described Congressional debates as "...frequently vague and perplexed and that they seem to drag their slow length along rather than to advance towards a distinct object."

Washington from the White House in the 1830s

174

Raisin' Cain

In the early years of the Union, passionate debates among members of Congress sometimes led to physical violence. In 1832, Congressman William Stanbery accused Samuel Houston of embezzling funds while acting as a government agent for the Cherokee tribe. After bumping into him on a Washington street, Houston attacked Stanbery with his cane. The case was brought before the House of Representatives. Houston defended himself so eloquently that he received a mere slap on the wrist, and the incident propelled him into the public light. One year later Houston went to Texas and led the war of independence against Mexico.

Silhouette of President Andrew Jackson, circa 1845

President Andrew Jackson had them to the White House for a glass of Madeira wine. Beaumont described Jackson as "an old man of 66 years, well preserved, and appears to have retained all the vigour of his body and spirit. He is not a man of genius."

Andrew Jackson and the presidency did not overly impress Tocqueville and Beaumont. Tocqueville wrote in *Democracy in America* that the office of the President, "has but little power, little wealth, and little glory to share among his friends ..."

The Frenchmen spent their days attending congressional sessions, listening to debates and discussing issues and ideals of democracy with friends and acquaintances.

Their minds, however, were elsewhere; despite the many distractions Washington offered, Beaumont thought only of his return to France. Tocqueville concentrated on what he would write about America. "One might be able...by selecting the topics, to present only those subjects having a more or less direct relation to our social and political state...the work might have...a permanent and an immediate interest," he wrote to his father. Perhaps this work would make his mark. "You say in one of your letters, dear Father, that you are counting on me to do something worth while in the world. I want to justify your expectation even more for your sake, I swear, than for my own."

In 1835, three years after their return to France, Beaumont wrote *Marie*, a novel about slavery in America, and Tocqueville published the first volume of *Democracy in America*.

A 21-foot statue of Albert Einstein sits almost hidden behind a grove of elm and holly trees at the National Academy of Sciences at 2101 Constitution Avenue. At Einstein's feet lies a 28-foot circular sky map of the known universe.

The U.S. Capitol

U.S. Capitol
In *Democracy in America,*
Tocqueville wrote, "They have
erected a magnificent palace for
Congress in the center of the city
and have given it the pompous
name of the Capitol." Today
visitors can take a 30-minute
tour of the center of the federal
government and listen to the
latest debates in Congress. The
halls of the building are
brilliantly painted with historical
scenes. Statuary Hall, the Old
Senate Chamber and the Old
Supreme Court Chamber are all
open for tours. The view from
the Capitol's west terrace is
spectacular. East end of the Mall.
Tel: (202) 225-6827.

Library of Congress
These three buildings house the
largest library in the world. The
Main Reading Room of the
Jefferson Building with its striking
dome is open to the public.
101 Independence Avenue, SE.
Tel: (202) 707-5000.

**Washington National
Cathedral**
Adorned with flying buttresses
and brilliant stained-glass windows
and guarded by comical
gargoyles and grotesques, the
cathedral is the sixth largest in
the world. Don't miss the secluded
Bishop's Garden and Herb
Garden which are adjacent to the
church. Massachusetts and
Wisconsin Avenues.
Tel: (202) 537-6200.

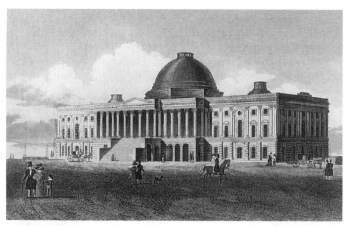

United States Capitol in the 1830s

Smithsonian "Castle" Building

Smithsonian Institution

The world's largest museum complex, the Smithsonian Institution consists of more than a dozen museums, galleries and the National Zoo. Many of the museums are situated along the National Mall.

The **Arthur M. Sackler Gallery** contains Asian and Near Eastern art.
1050 Independence Avenue, SW.
Tel: (202) 357-2700.

The **Arts and Industries Building** houses an array of American memorabilia.
900 Jefferson Drive, SW.
Tel: (202) 357-2700.

The **Freer Gallery of Art** features Asian and 19th- to 20th-century American art.
Jefferson Drive at 12th Street, SW.
Tel: (202) 357-2700.

The **Hirshhorn Museum and Sculpture Garden** houses modern art. Outside, the sculpture garden displays 19th- and 20th-century statues along winding paths.
Independence Avenue at 7th Street, SW.
Tel: (202) 357-2700.

The **National Air and Space Museum**, one of the most popular museums on the Mall, tells the story of flight from the Wright Brothers to the *Apollo 11* and features aircraft including the *Enola Gay,* which dropped the atomic bomb on Hiroshima, Japan.
Independence Avenue at 7th Street, SW.
Tel: (202) 357-2700.

The **National Museum of African Art** has a collection of 6,000 works of traditional African arts. 950 Independence Avenue, SW.
Tel: (202) 357-2700.

The **National Museum of American Art** has a diverse collection of art by American masters. 8th and G Streets, NW.
Tel: (202) 357-2700.

The **National Museum of American History** depicts America's past including an exploration of the roots of slavery and displays focused on American inventions. George Washington's wooden teeth and Dorothy's

177

The Lincoln Memorial

The **National Postal Museum** recounts the country's postal history and contains a large collection of historic stamps. 2 Massachusetts Avenue, NE. Tel: (202) 357-2700.

American crafts are honored at the **Renwick Gallery** which has a collection of 20th-century decorative arts. 17th Street and Pennsylvania Avenue, NW. Tel: (202) 357-2700.

The White House
The most visited house in the world, the White House has been home to every president except George Washington. The first to live at 1600 Pennsylvania Avenue were John and Abigail Adams. The Green Room, the Red Room, the Blue Room, the State Dining Room and the East Room are open to the public. To tour the house visitors need to reserve tickets in advance. Tickets are issued on the day of the tour and are available on a first-come-first-serve basis. 1600 Pennsylvania Avenue. Tel: (202) 456-7041.

Ford's Theatre
The theater where Abraham Lincoln was assassinated on April 14, 1865, looks much as it did on that fatal night and is still in operation. Downstairs is a museum which depicts the shooting and exhibits the gun John Wilkes Booth used to kill Lincoln. 511 10th Street, NW. Tel: (202) 426-6924.

Decatur House Museum
Built for U.S. naval hero Stephen Decatur and designed by Benjamin Latrobe, an architect who worked on the U.S. Capitol, the Decatur House was once a

ruby slippers are housed here. Constitution Avenue between 12th and 14th streets. Tel: (202) 357-2700.

A huge African bush elephant greets visitors at the **National Museum of Natural History** which has a wide collection including exhibits on dinosaurs, sharks and gems. Look for the renowned blue Hope Diamond. Constitution Avenue at 10th Street, NW. Tel: (202) 357-2700.

At the **National Portrait Gallery** find more than 11,000 paintings, photographs and sculptures of people who have contributed to the culture of the United States. 8th and F Streets, NW. Tel: (202) 357-2700.

Eastern Market on 7th and C Streets, SE, sells fresh vegetables, meats and cheeses in its historic brick market building. On weekends dealers sell crafts and antiques outside.

178

center for Washington society and a gathering place for politicians. The house is decorated with period furnishings.
1600 H Street, NW.
Tel: (202) 842-0920.

Monuments

Located in the heart of the National Mall, the **Washington Monument** obelisk soars more than 550 feet high. Visitors can acquire a ticket to walk up the 897 steps for a panoramic view of the city.
Constitution Avenue at 15th Street.
Tel: (202) 426-6841.

At the base of the Reflecting Pool sits the **Lincoln Memorial,** where in August of 1963, Dr. Martin Luther King, Jr. gave his *I Have A Dream* speech to 250,000 supporters. Inside, a statue of Abraham Lincoln is flanked by engravings of his most famous speeches: the Gettysburg Address and his Second Inaugural Address. 23rd Street between Constitution and Independence Avenues, NW.
Tel: (202) 426-6841.

The **Thomas Jefferson Memorial,** located at the foot of the Tidal Basin, is surrounded by white and pink cherry blossoms in the spring.
15th Street, SW on the Tidal Basin.
Tel: (202) 426-6821.

The long, polished, black granite wall of the **Vietnam Veterans Memorial** contains more than 58,000 names of those who died or remain missing in the war.
Constitution Avenue and Henry Bacon Drive.
Tel: (202) 426-6841.

The **Korean War Veterans Memorial,** with its 7-foot-tall statues of combat-ready soldiers, is located near the Lincoln Memorial.

Independence Avenue and Daniel French Drive.
Tel: (202) 426-6841.

One of the newest memorials, the **Franklin Delano Roosevelt Memorial** is situated among waterfalls with bronze sculptures depicting the life of Roosevelt. Along Cherry Tree Walk at the Tidal Basin. Tel: (202) 426- 6841.

Washington, DC
Today

More than 500,000 people live in the city proper and even more work here. Washington is made up of many diverse neighborhoods including Georgetown with its Federal-style brownstones, shops,

The Washington Monument

restaurants and boutiques. The Georgetown Harbor provides an impressive view of the Kennedy Center and offers riverside dining. Capitol Hill is the site of many government buildings and restored townhouses. Union Station, located near Capitol Hill, is a Beaux Arts train station featuring shops and restaurants. Adams Morgan is a blend of ethnic restaurants and trendy nightclubs. The city's clean Metro subway system stops at many downtown attractions.

Inns and Outs

How to get there:
From the north take I-95 south to I-295 and exit at Pennsylvania Avenue. From the south take I-95 north to I-395 north and exit at the 14th Street Bridge.

Where to stay:
For lodging information contact the Washington, DC Convention and Visitors Association. 1212 New York Avenue, NW, Suite 600, Washington, DC 20005. Tel: (202) 789-7000.

Other Attractions

United States Holocaust Memorial Museum
This museum memorializes the annihilation of the six million Jewish people who died during World War II. There is no cost to visit the museum but tickets are required. 100 Raoul Wallenberg Place, SW. Tel: (202) 488-0400.

The Phillips Collection
This museum houses a prized collection of 19th- and 20th-century art, including popular impressionist works such as Pierre-Auguste Renoir's *Luncheon of the Boating Party*. 1600 21st Street, NW. Tel: (202) 387-2151.

National Zoo
Part of the Smithsonian Institution, the National Zoo is famous for its giant panda. Indoor and outdoor exhibits house hundreds of animals. 3001 Connecticut Avenue, NW. Tel: (202) 673-4800.

Mount Vernon
George Washington's home sits high above the Potomac River just a few miles from Washington, DC, in Virginia on the George Washington Parkway. The house is decorated with period furnishings and includes the bed where Washington died, his sword and a key to the Bastille which was presented to him by the Marquis de Lafayette. 3200 Mount Vernon Memorial Highway. Tel: (703) 780-2000.

Arlington National Cemetery
Established in 1864 on Robert E. Lee's land and located across the Potomac in Virginia, Arlington National Cemetery is the burial ground for some of America's most famous soldiers and statespersons. Memorial Drive, across the Memorial Bridge from Washington, DC. Tel: (703) 697-2131.

180

ALEXIS DE TOCQUEVILLE

The 25 year-old French aristocrat
and author of

Democracy in America

visited this area
during his 1831-1832 tour of America

Tocqueville
C-SPAN

PLACED BY C-SPAN AND THE CABLE TELEVISION INDUSTRY
while retracing the tour in 1997-1998

Acknowledgments

C-SPAN would like to thank the following cable companies for hosting the C-SPAN School Bus on the Tocqueville Tour.

Newport, Rhode Island
Cox Communications—
West Warwick, Rhode Island

New York City, New York
Time Warner Cable—
New York City, New York

Ossining, New York
MediaOne—
Ossining, New York

Greenburgh, New York
TCI—
Mamaroneck, New York

Yonkers, New York
Cablevision Systems—
Yonkers, New York

Peekskill, New York
MediaOne—
Ossining, New York

Newburgh, New York
Time Warner Cable—
Newburgh, New York

Albany, New York
Time Warner Cable—
Albany, New York

Utica, New York
Harron Communications—
Utica, New York

Syracuse, New York
Adelphia Cable
Communications—
Syracuse, New York

Fort Brewerton, New York
Time Warner Cable—
Syracuse, New York

Auburn, New York
Auburn Cablevision—
Auburn, New York

Canandaigua, New York
Time Warner Cable—
Geneva, New York

Batavia, New York
Time Warner Cable—
Batavia, New York

Buffalo, New York
TCI—
Buffalo, New York

Erie, Pennsylvania
Erie Cablevision—
Erie, Pennsylvania

Cleveland, Ohio
Cablevision Systems—
Cleveland, Ohio

Detroit, Michigan
Comcast Cablevision—
Detroit, Michigan

Pontiac, Michigan
Comcast Cablevision—
Waterford, Michigan

Flint, Michigan
Comcast Cablevision—
Detroit, Michigan

Saginaw, Michigan
TCI—
Saginaw, Michigan

Fort Gratiot, Michigan
Harron Communications—
Port Huron, Michigan

Sault Ste. Marie, Michigan
Bresnan Communications—
Sault Ste. Marie, Michigan

Mackinac Island, Michigan
Bresnan Communications—
Sault Ste. Marie, Michigan

Green Bay, Wisconsin
Time Warner Cable—
Kimberly, Wisconsin

Niagara Falls, New York
Adelphia Cable
Communications—
Niagara Falls, New York

Whitehall, New York
Time Warner Cable—
Glens Falls, New York

Stockbridge, Massachusetts
Century Communications—
Lee, Massachusetts

Boston, Massachusetts
Cablevision Systems—
Brookline, Massachusetts

Hartford, Connecticut
TCI—
Hartford, Connecticut

Wethersfield, Connecticut
Cox Communications—
Manchester, Connecticut

Philadelphia, Pennsylvania
Comcast Cablevision—
Philadelphia, Pennsylvania

Philadelphia, Pennsylvania
Greater Media Cable—
Philadelphia, Pennsylvania

Baltimore, Maryland
TCI—
Baltimore, Maryland

Pittsburgh, Pennsylvania
TCI—
Pittsburgh, Pennsylvania

Wheeling, West Virginia
TCI—
Bridgeport, Ohio

Cincinnati, Ohio
Time Warner Cable—
Cincinnati, Ohio

Westport, Kentucky
Insight Communications—
Jeffersonville, Indiana

Louisville, Kentucky
TKR Cable—
Louisville, Kentucky

Nashville, Tennessee
InterMedia Cable—
Nashville, Tennessee

Memphis, Tennessee
Time Warner Cable—
Memphis, Tennessee

New Orleans, Louisiana
Cox Communications—
New Orleans, Louisiana

Mobile, Alabama
Comcast Cablevision—
Mobile, Alabama

Montgomery, Alabama
TCI—
Montgomery, Alabama

Knoxville, Georgia
Flint Cable TV—
Reynolds, Georgia

Macon, Georgia
Cox Communications—
Macon, Georgia

Milledgeville, Georgia
InterMedia Cable—
Milledgeville, Georgia

Augusta, Georgia
Jones Intercable—
Augusta, Georgia

Columbia, South Carolina
Time Warner Cable—
West Columbia, South Carolina

Fayetteville, North Carolina
Time Warner Cable—
Fayetteville, North Carolina

Norfolk, Virginia
Cox Communications/
Hampton Roads—
Virginia Beach, Virginia

Washington, DC
District Cablevision—
Washington, DC

Acknowledgments

Many scholars and historians helped with the research for C-SPAN's Tocqueville Tour and the compilation of this book. Both the tour and the book could not have happened without their enthusiastic work and expert knowledge of history, political thought and Alexis de Tocqueville. While the list is too long to name each individually, there are a few people who deserve special thanks: Roger Boesche of Occidental College; James Ceaser of the University of Virginia; Seymour Drescher of the University of Pittsburgh; Peter Lawler of Berry College; Daniel J. Mahoney of Assumption College; Harvey Mansfield of Harvard University; Ken Masugi of USAF Academy; Edna Medford of Howard University; Francoise Melonio; Alan Ryan of Princeton University; Jim Schleifer of the College of New Rochelle; Delba Winthrop of Harvard University; Catherine Zuckert of Carleton College; and Olivier Zunz of the University of Virginia.

Town historians provided detailed information and illustrations for this book under unusually tight deadlines. C-SPAN would like to especially thank the following historians for their research and assistance: Joan Youngkin; Roberta Arminio; Joanne Weinberg; Andrew Smith; John Curran; Virginia Kelly; Stephanie E. Przybylek; Thomas Eldrid; Jack Frost; Mark J. Koziol; Dennis J. Conners; Linda McIlveen; Sue Conklin; Dennis Farmer; Anita Andreck; Sandra Vodanoff; Charlie Martinez; Steve Weikal; Stephen Williams; Nancy Sharon; Donald Gerrie; Susan Shocker; Len Trankina; Phil Porter; Carol Greenough; Polly Pierce; Gary E. Wait; Brenda Milkofsky; David Dashiell; Charles Duff; Anne McDonnell; Ophelia Payne; Ray Sigmond; Joe Moser; and Richard Salzberg.

Credits

Alabama Department of Archives and History: p.152. Albany County Convention and Visitors Bureau: p.28; p.30/Albany Urban Cultural Park; p.31a plaza rink; p.31b capitol. Albany Institute of History and Art: p.27. Louie Anderson: p.54. Auburn Chamber of Commerce: p.40b stained-glass window. Augusta Metropolitan Convention and Visitors Bureau: p.163b cotton center and museum; p.164. Donnie Beauchamp: p.138. Buffalo and Erie County Historical Society: p.45. Charles Burton: p.114b penitentiary. Burton Historical Collection of the Detroit Public Library: p.56. Ron Calamia: p.147b sax player; p.148. Carnegie Library of Pittsburgh: p.121. Catskill Marina: p.25. Cayuga County Historical Society: p.38; p.41. Columbia Metropolitan Convention and Visitors Bureau: pp.166-167. Connecticut Historical Society, Hartford: p.104. C-SPAN: p.74b locks; p.135. The Chrysler Museum of Art: p.170. Delta Queen Steamboat Company: p.134. Detroit Historical Museum: p.61. Dover Pictorial Archive Series: p.129. Alastair Duncan: p.29. Erie Area Convention and Visitors Bureau: p.49. Fayetteville Area Convention and Visitors Bureau: pp.168-169. Flint Area Convention and Visitors Bureau: pp.64-65. Genesee County Historical Society: p.47. Greater Boston Convention and Visitors Bureau: p.100; pp.102-103. Greater Buffalo Convention and Visitors Bureau: p.46/Mary Dawes; p.48/Mary Dawes. Greater Cincinnati Convention and Visitors Bureau: p.130; p.131/George Soister, Graphic Concepts of Cincinnati. Greater Hartford Tourism District: p.108; p.109a meeting house and church; p.109b warehouse. Greater Montreal Convention and Tourism Bureau: pp.86-89. Greater Pittsburgh Convention and Visitors Bureau: p.122/Jeff Greenberg; p.123a skyline/M.G. Ellis; p.123b neighborhood/Jeff Greenberg; p.124/M.G. Ellis. Greater Quebec Area Tourism and Convention Bureau: p.91; pp.93-94. Historic Hudson Valley: p.17/Steve Turner; p.18a Irving's study/Ted Spiegel; p.18b Sunnyside/David Forbert; p.19a Chagall window/Ted Spiegel; p.19b Kykuit/Ping Amranand; p.26/Tom O'Connell. The Historic New Orleans Collection: p.145. Historical Society of Pennsylvania: p.111. Robin Hood: p.137; p.139. Elizabeth Jackson: p.12a skyline; p.15; p.16b State Street. Jeff Jerome: p.118. Johns Hopkins University Press: p.3; p.20; p.35; p.66; p.75; p.78; p.81; p.90; p.92; p.98b church; pp.125-126. Lande Collection of Canadiana, Rare Books and Special Collections Department, McGill University, Montreal: p.85. Leisure Management Memphis: p.143a arena. Margret Lloyd: p.84a falls; p.110. Jack Long: p.14. Mackinac Island Chamber of Commerce: p.76a Skull Cave/Terry W. Phipps; p.76b Grand Hotel/Terry W. Phipps; p.77a Mackinac Island/Terry W. Phipps; p.77b Fort Mackinac/Terry W. Phipps. Macon-Bibb County Convention and Visitors Bureau: p.157; p.158a festival; p.158b hall of fame. Mariano Advertising: p.147a king. Kiersten Marshall: p.4a White Horse; p.4b tavern. Massachusetts Historical Society: p.99/Asher B. Durand. Jim McElholm: pp.5-7; pp.106-107. Jim McWilliams: p.115. Memphis Convention and Visitors Bureau: pp.141-142; p.143b museum; p.144. Metropolitan Detroit Convention and Visitors Bureau: pp.58-59. Middle Georgia Archives, Washington Memorial Library: p.156. Middleton Evans Photography: pp.119-120. Milledgeville-Baldwin County Convention and Visitors Bureau: pp.159-161. Andrew Peter Miller: p.181. Mobile Convention and Visitors Corporation: p.150; p.151a Oakleigh; p.151b Gunner's Room. Montgomery Area Chamber of Commerce: p.154a White House; p.154b church; p.155. Nashville Convention and Visitors Bureau: p.140/David Wright. National Portrait Gallery: p.50. New York Convention and Visitors Bureau: p.10; p.12b museum; p.13. New York Historical Society: p.8/H.Reinagle. New York Public Library/Gansevoort-Lansing Collection: p.34. Niagara Department of Planning, Development & Tourism: p.83b Maid of the Mist. Niagara Frontier State

A Note on Sources

Historical information and quotations from the letters and writings of Alexis de Tocqueville and Gustave de Beaumont found in this book are drawn from *Journey to America,* translated by George Lawrence and edited by J. P. Mayer (Westport: Greenwood Press, 1981); *Tocqueville in America,* by George Wilson Pierson (Baltimore: Johns Hopkins University Press, 1996); and Alexis de Tocqueville's *Democracy in America* (available in various editions).